LUMINOUS

THE SIERRA NEVADA OF CALIFORNIA

Yosemite Association, Yosemite National Park, California

M O U N T A I N S

P H O T O G R A P H S   A N D   T E X T   B Y   T I M   P A L M E R

HEYDAY BOOKS, BERKELEY, CALIFORNIA

Library of Congress Cataloging-in-Publication Data
Palmer, Tim, 1948-
Luminous mountains : the Sierra Nevada of California /
photographs and text by Tim Palmer.
p. cm.
Includes bibliographical references and index.
ISBN-13: 978-1-59714-077-5 (pbk. : alk. paper)
1. Sierra Nevada (Calif. and Nev.)—Pictorial works.
2. Sierra Nevada (Calif. and Nev.)—Description and travel.
3. Palmer, Tim, 1948—Travel—Sierra Nevada (Calif. and Nev.)
4. Hiking—Sierra Nevada (Calif. and Nev.)
5. Natural history—Sierra Nevada (Calif. and Nev.)
6. Sierra Nevada (Calif. and Nev.) Environmental conditions. I.Title.
F868.S5P35 2008
917.94´40454—dc22   2007025186

Cover Photo: A golden sunrise glows on Lone Pine Peak while
autumn snowfall dusts northeast slopes.

Maps Designed by: Cartagram, LLC.
Cover and Interior Design and Typesetting: David Bullen

Orders, inquiries, and correspondence
should be addressed to:
Heyday Books
P. O. Box 9145, Berkeley, CA 94709
(510) 549-3564, Fax (510) 549-1889
www.heydaybooks.com

Printed in Singapore by Imago

10   9   8   7   6   5   4   3   2   1

In memory of Steve Medley —Yosemite Association leader and guide, husband, father, publisher, author, visionary friend of mine, and one of the finest advocates the Sierra Nevada ever had

MOUNT TOM AND BASIN MOUNTAIN
Mount Tom reaches to 13,652 feet at the eastern escarpment of the Sierra, with Basin Mountain (bottom of photo) to its south.

page 1
VOLUNTEER PEAK
In northern Yosemite National Park, the sun illumines remaining clouds after an evening thunderstorm.

pages 2–3
TUOLUMNE RIVER
The Tuolumne crests in a massive wave of early summer runoff at the brink of Glen Aulin Falls.

pages 4–5
MOUNT HUMPHREYS AND THE EASTERN SIERRA
High on the Sierra crest west of Bishop, Mount Humphreys (right of center) and nearby peaks begin to warm with the first rays of a new day.

page 8
FOXTAIL PINES IN THE GOLDEN TROUT WILDERNESS
Ancient in their isolation among granite boulders near Cottonwood Lakes, foxtail pines grace high-elevation slopes of the southern Sierra.

page 9 top left
MULE DEER AT YOSEMITE
Mule deer live throughout the Sierra. Because the deer spend summers in the high mountains and travel down to the foothills for winter range, habitat along their entire migration corridor is important for the herds' survival.

page 9 top right
CENTAURIUM VENUSTUM
In the East Fork Carson River Canyon, these "charming centaury" brighten the forest floor in July.

page 9 bottom
MERCED RIVER AT VERNAL FALL
The Merced River foams over Vernal Fall, just upstream from Yosemite Valley.

page 10 top
RED FIRS AT BASIN PEAK
A high-elevation red fir forest reaches its limits at the windswept timberline of Basin Peak, north of Donner Pass.

page 10 bottom
OLD-GROWTH FOREST AT YUBA PASS
Lichen-covered red firs form a magnificent grove near Yuba Pass, in the northern Sierra. Large trees and undisturbed forests are important to whole communities of wildlife, to the quality of water supplies, to the control of wildfires, and to the maintenance of our climate. However, less than 25 percent of the Sierra's old-growth forest remains uncut.

page 11
SIERRA FOOTHILLS AND OAK TREES
Blue oaks, canyon live oaks, and annual grasses green springtime foothills in the Merced basin. Low-elevation habitat such as this is critical to many species of wildlife.

CONTENTS

BANNER PEAK

In windless, early morning light, Banner
Peak is reflected in Thousand Island Lake.

Enchanted by what lay before me, I watched the mountains loom larger and larger on the horizon. The simplicity of a distant sky-line gradually took on complexity with crags and scarps, with snow-fields glazed by ice, and with a texture of rockiness evident from many miles away. The increasing clarity of the scene held me rapt, glued to the view.

Though for years I had steeped myself in pictures and stories about the Sierra Nevada, none of them prepared me for what was now about to happen.

Living out a young man's dreams at that time, 1968, I was hitch-hiking to California. From out in the desert I could see the first rise of the mythic land in the highest ridge that marked the Sierra crest. I rode with a congenial schoolteacher, who was on his way to Yosemite National Park.

As we speeded closer and closer to the rugged slopes and saw-toothed peaks, the distant view of the range as a monolithic whale of geography disappeared; we had entered the mountains themselves and felt their tight embrace of landform. Instead of the big, sweeping, wide-angled view, scenes of delectable intimacy emerged—a waterfall here,

a wind-sculpted conifer there; a white cliff face fractured with black cracks, a pillow of willows mounded at water's edge.

The curving highway going up Lee Vining Canyon drew us further, and though we climbed toward Tioga Pass with each banked bend in the road, I had the distinct feeling of going not so much higher but rather deeper into the folds of warping rock, deeper into the forests of lodgepole pine, deeper into the glacial enclaves once buried in ice but now drowned in pure luminous light so rich it seemed drinkable in yellow and gold.

I couldn't stand it any longer.

"Let me out here," I said.

I had read the writings of John Muir, who came here as a young man, loved the mountains, wrote and spoke eloquently for their preservation, and launched the first movement to protect nature and wilderness in America. Now I knew that the ebullient naturalist really meant what he wrote, every single word of it.

Each rock caught my eye with its own sharpness of form, yet its dependence on other rocks was obvious, all piled up there together as they were. Stepping from boulder to boulder, I had only the simplest of thoughts. "This is what makes up the Sierra Nevada—one rock on top of another." No less, I saw that the range was made of trees that swayed together as a forest, of snowmelt rivulets that flowed together as a stream, of myriad life-forms together relying on the wildness of the land around them. I spotted the Clark's nutcracker, a flashy, noisy bird darting in and out of clusters of pines. I knew that other, more cautious eyes were likely watching me, and that they might be those of such evolutionary marvels as the peregrine falcon, black bear, and mountain lion. I vaguely but intuitively realized that all these elements—earth,

15

LANGILLE PEAK
With granite monoliths, spires, and domes, the walls of LeConte Canyon tower over the Middle Fork of the Kings River.

water, life—were interwoven and dependent on each other no less than the rocks underfoot that would tip or roll beneath my feet if they lacked the support of the rocks next to them.

America's greatest granite batholith jutted skyward to the peaks, some sharp and pointed, some round and domed, all drawing my eyes and imagination upward. I understood the irresistible impulse to climb. I felt it in my muscles and bones. The peaks topped out at heights unimaginable from my Appalachian perspective, but I was ready to go, ready to open the door to a whole new world and to whole new ways of looking at a world that I had thought I knew, but didn't.

Colliding at times with the white and gray granite summits, clouds of the same colors drifted past whimsically with crisply etched tops and damp dark bottoms—just enough substance to tell me that the weather, the wind, and the sky were no less important to the extravagant makeup of this place than were the rocks that gave the earth its shape under my feet. One dark cloud caused me to wonder, briefly, "Is there anything to fear?" But the beauty of the place was far too great, and I quickly dismissed the thought.

Like a little dog scenting out multiple trails on the ground around him, I was drawn in different directions by the intricate lay of the land— an opening here, a passageway there, a border of lupine followed by a ledge where I could step out to the brink and feel the exhilaration of

16

LAKE TAHOE
The sun sets at Lake Tahoe State Park in Nevada. The extraordinary water quality of this second-deepest lake in America is deteriorating because of land development and air pollution.

resounding empty space—not just air above me, and in front of me, but air below me as well. Backing off from the edge, I strolled a short distance, dropped my pack in the grass, and wandered farther with no load to carry.

The sound of water—which always before had enticed me down into hollows and lowland valleys—now lured me up to where crystal-clear runoff sprayed refreshment from the edge of an alpine waterfall. With whole new desires being stirred in my heart, I was pulled onward to the top of a boulder that offered a beautiful prospect toward both the valley below and the peaks above. Looking out over it all, I felt a hint of strangely unlimited opportunity, though I couldn't define it or even tell what the emotion truly was. Along with this pleasantly unsettling surge in my heart, I felt that I belonged—I felt intrinsically a part of nature's workings that thrived all around me. Yet I was certain that I didn't know enough about those mountains to truly belong. That would have to come later.

My short introduction to the Sierra Nevada whetted my appetite for more. I wanted to climb a peak for the sheer fun and adventure of it, but also to see what the mountains and what the rest of California looked like from up there. As I watched the stream foaming down to lower ground, I wondered what it would be like to travel with the waters of the Sierra. How many rivers drained this country? I had no idea, but I suspected that each offered a unique way to experience the mountains by traveling on the flush of pure runoff that inevitably follows the deep accumulation of snow in winter.

And what would the mountains be like then, when storms drop two, four, six feet of snow at a time? As I stood in the sun on that balmy August day, the frigid blizzards and deepening drifts seemed as distant as the Pleistocene, but nonetheless I knew that winter is the dominant season in the Sierra. High-country lakes don't thaw until June; to know the mountains means knowing them in the dark, cold, snowy months. I thought that someday—maybe someday—I could explore the range in winter. Maybe I could even stay for a while, just to watch the snow fall and to see it grow deeper and deeper all around me.

I realized that I was seeing only one small piece of the Sierra Nevada, and I dreamed of launching a truly epic journey. What would it be like to walk for hundreds of miles through these mountains? How could I arrange for such a trip—one that would truly immerse me in all that was wild and natural about this great range of rock, forest, water, weather, life?

I knew, then, that one could spend a lifetime exploring the Sierra. I concluded that this would be a lifetime well spent.

Stepping out into those mountains on that brilliant summer day, I sensed that I was starting an important new chapter in the book of my life.

On that first trip to the Sierra, I wanted to see it all, and now, thirty-eight years later, I still do.

Back then, I couldn't get enough, and now, half a lifetime later, I still can't.

Now realizing that I will never explore the whole range, I enjoy reflecting on the parts that I've been lucky enough to see. But no matter how fortunate I've been, I can't help wanting to see more in the precious years to come, beginning right now, today, beginning right here, once again, as I step onto the trail. With high expectations, I anticipate the beauty that will appear on the path in front of me—a path that will take me to wonders as great as any I enjoyed on that hitchhiking trip years ago when I first entered the Sierra Nevada and said, with a deeply satisfying sense of certainty, "Let me out here."

Searching for the best view, I climbed steadily before the sun beamed up over the Sierra Nevada crest to the east. The mix of granite bedrock, tumbling stream, and pine-scented forest propelled me onward, each scene tempting me with a finely detailed foreground that made me want to look closer and an intriguing background that made me want to look farther.

High above the rim of the glacial cirque that artistically contained my world for the moment, Pyramid Peak rose up to the sky.

Dawn had broken cool, crisp, and promising. With just enough food for a few days, and nominal gear, I traveled light, enjoying the tingling feeling of freedom that comes whenever I sever my tie with roads.

Pines, firs, and cedars transpired into the same air that I breathed, and the scent of the conifers prompted me to take a deeper breath. The air was sweetened so freshly that it stirred thoughts of new beginnings of many kinds. Breathing forest air, especially in the Sierra Nevada, makes me feel like it's the first day of life. All the rest is out ahead of me, waiting to be seen, waiting to be encountered, waiting to be felt.

The smell of the evergreens was terrific, but not to be outdone in a tough competition for my senses, Pyramid Creek rushed toward me with stereophonic sound. Up ahead, its healthy flow of early summer snowmelt formed one of the larger and more dazzling waterfalls in the Sierra as it jetted off the high rim of granite, pummeled several clefts of rock on the way down, and free-fell onto piles of white glistening rubble before being tamed into moderate chutes, rapids, and ledge-drops leading to the South Fork of the American River. Distant rumbles of the falls, along with the bubbling of the stream nearby, all harmonized from different chairs in the orchestra. The water music filled an otherwise quiet morning now that the highly forgettable road-noise of Highway 50 lay far below.

My destination was the top of Pyramid Peak. I wanted a good climb for the special feeling that comes only with the unquestionable climax of reaching the top, yet I didn't want to face the hazards that come with a seriously demanding ascent. Of course, little that's worth doing is risk-free, but this climb presented few of the complications that so easily arise in rugged mountain country. Or so I hoped.

Many Sierra Nevada peaks are safe enough for a well-prepared person to walk up alone, but I also wanted a summit of great prospect. Among the many reasons I go to the mountains, the most fundamental is to see. Simply stated, I love to see the earth, and mountaintops provide for quite a view.

I had been hiking in the Sierra for many years, but as I began writing and photographing for this book, I wanted to reestablish a new sense of beginning. I now had my mind on the whole Sierra, not just isolated parts. I wanted to look across the breadth and length of the mountains as much as possible, to see the range's lay-of-land, to recognize its position relative to all that touches it and to all that lies beyond.

Pyramid, I reasoned, would fit the bill because it stands nearly isolated

Pyramid Peak
A landmark of the northern Sierra, Pyramid Peak presides over the Desolation Wilderness and can be seen from Sacramento on days when air pollution or clouds don't obscure the view. Mount Price caps the skyline to the right.

above its surroundings, clearly the crown of the Sierra Nevada within its region. Just from the map, I could see that no other mountain obstructs Pyramid's view across the entire 180-degree sweep of geography to the west—the window to the rest of California. This quirk of location makes Pyramid a landmark from countrysides, towns, and cities below, including Sacramento, where I had once happily lived off and on for several years. On one of the increasingly rare clear days there in the state capital, the mountains look like a gleaming white ocean wave, sixty miles away. This is the Sierra subgroup fittingly called the Crystal Range, and the symmetrical, southernmost summit that tops all others is Pyramid.

I had seen it many times from a distance, and now I wanted to be there, to know what the place was really like, to feel its rocks under my boots, to smell the air given off by its forests, to hear the voice of the mountain through all the language it speaks—rocks clattering, water bubbling, wind whistling. And who knew what else I would hear?

The view to the west would be open, but to its north, east, and south, Pyramid faced rugged terrain. In those directions I suspected that I would see a long, continuous reach of the greater range and find evidence of the hidden powers that make the Sierra Nevada what it is.

Seismic forces built the mountains up, and by an estimated one-third of a millimeter per year they continue to push the crest higher. That doesn't sound like much, but over the millennia it adds up to some of the highest mountains in the coterminous United States. The granite batholith that defines the Sierra was formed from molten, igneous mineral masses that cooled slowly while underground. That process resulted in the coarse-grained, light-colored rock that characterizes much of the twenty-million-acre expanse of the range, counting from the toe of the western foothills to the base of the eastern slope. Along with plentiful infusions of volcanic rubble and a spicy mix of sedimentary and metamorphic rocks showing in multi-colored cake layers, the whole mass rose many thousands of feet through earthquake activity. This results indirectly from the slippage of the North American continental plate against the Pacific plate, and also with the rifting of topography in the massive Great Basin, which lies to the east.

Squeezed by all these forces, the Sierra Nevada is fractured by fault lines. A diagram of them looks like badly broken glass. The dominant thrust, however, pushes upward on the east side where the rock emerges out of the ground, leaving a steep escarpment. A more gentle western slope coasts down to the Central Valley, which lies almost at sea level. The whole range reminds me of an ocean swell, approaching from the Pacific and about to break. Pyramid Peak describes a smaller wind-tossed wave atop that giant swell, a sign of real turbulence among the most powerful forces of creation, whether they be winds across the ocean or seismic upheaval across the land.

As the longest continuous mass of unbroken high country in the forty-eight states, the Sierra Nevada stretches four hundred miles from its northern coupling with the Cascade Range near Mount Lassen to Tehachapi Pass in the south, where the Sierra abuts the Tehachapi Mountains—one of southern California's five transverse ranges aligned east-west and extending out to the Pacific.

These crucial facts of geography determine everything else that follows. Being mountains, the Sierra Nevada forces the prevailing westerly winds to rise up over it, and when that happens, the wet storms of winter are cooled, and they drop rain and snow in immense quantities. This gift of the mountains not only nourishes all the life of the Sierra but serves as the primary water supply for most of California and its major cities.

The rugged topography of mountain environments is difficult to travel through, to build roads across, to develop, to farm, and even to log or mine. Thus, with limited accessibility, and with a heritage of environmental protection stronger than in most other places, the Sierra has remained less affected by civilization. Wildlife takes refuge from the encroachments that have decimated habitat and eliminated entire species down below. For the same reasons, the Sierra offers an escape for people seeking solace, excitement, or separation from the urban drone of California, our most populous state.

At the base of Pyramid Creek's great waterfall, I began to climb in

earnest. Aside from random paths taken by other hikers, there is no real trail up this route, and so I stepped from one rock to another, strode across granite slabs tilted to the limit of my traction, and occasionally clutched skinny trunks of pines and cedars, which clung to bare rocks with tenacity and thrift I couldn't imagine. Now and then I gripped edges of rock, wedged the toe of a boot into a crack in the granite, and pulled my weight forcibly up to the next level. I traversed to the right until I came to the curved face of granite, smoothed out by the waterfall as if by a spatula on the inside of a great mixing bowl. Then I doubled back to the left until I came to a wall too steep to climb. I sought the path of least resistance, though mountains offer resistance everywhere and might well be defined as the path of most resistance.

When I reached the top of the waterfall, the terrain eased into gentler high country decorated with boulders plunked down erratically by the migrating glaciers. Lakes glimmered in multiple tiers, as if whole terraces of granite had been flooded, one above another. Trees took on contorted shapes; they had been forced to withstand the high country's increasing severity of wind, snow, drift, cold, ice, sun, aridity, rockfall, avalanche.

Pyramid Peak rose as a monument above everything—just the kind of place I had been looking for. Long slopes of loose rubble lay at a steady angle of repose—the angle of steepness at which the stones stop falling and come to a temporary rest. Snowfields remained in drift lines where the winter winds had been checked by ridges and then had dropped their loads. Other slopes, where fearsome winter gusts had swept the mountain face clean even during the storms themselves, lay wholly exposed in rock.

Needing shelter for the night, I pitched my tent at the base of a west-facing slope that would catch the last light of the day. For the remainder of the afternoon I wandered across the granite bedrock, skirting the edge of Avalanche Lake, then Pitt Lake, then Ropi Lake. I rambled along picturesque streams that connected the lakes together.

Late in the afternoon I returned to camp and began cooking my dinner while the sun dropped and the light became warmly colored. I could see toward the canyons of Pyramid Creek and the South Fork

CENTRAL AND SOUTHERN SIERRA
The full width of the Sierra high country can be seen here stretching southward in a multitude of spectacular peaks. Formed by earthquakes, the range juts up sharply from the east and slopes more gradually to the Central Valley in the west. Humphreys Basin, west of Bishop, appears as a large white area in the upper left; air pollution from the southern Central Valley hazes western slopes in the background.

American, and I watched the sun dip lower near the western horizon. With each passing minute, the late-day light on my world grew more golden, and the continuing change fascinated me. What had been gray granite cliffs earlier now shone as if they were their own sources of light—luminous. I took a picture, realizing that capturing the essence of these mountains on film means capturing the essence of light.

Still staring at the sweet ripening of late-day color, I noticed that a chilling sunset shadow was creeping up toward me from the depths of the canyon. Inevitably the approaching darkness would signal the passing of a day I did not want to end. Yet the shadow seemed to move slowly, and I became intrigued with the notion of keeping ahead of it as it approached. Could I race the shadow up the slope to the east, prolonging the glow of sun in my eyes?

I dropped my dinner in mid-bite and began climbing.

Hustling quickly, straight up the inclined granite slope and then onto fell-fields of cascaded rock, I managed to stay in the golden light for a while, staving off sunset, delaying the end of the day with an eager burst of enthusiasm. But soon the alignment of mountains and canyon walls conspired against me and the shadow leaped suddenly upward, throwing me into deep shade and a chill that announced the coming of a starry night.

I walked slowly back down to camp, knowing that I had squeezed what I could out of the day. In many other places, it's easy to take the turning of the earth for granted, but in the Sierra, the quality of light signals something extraordinary each time the sun sets, and each time it rises again. When I reached camp, the day was gone, but I felt pleased with the simple promise that the light would return—that the cycle would go on. I wanted to see it, and to be a part of it, and to be a part of all the mountain cycles, not just tomorrow, but for years, and for life.

The next morning I set off early with a new spring in my step as I imagined the views to come. I skirted the shore of Avalanche Lake and then began to climb Pyramid, first wading through a tangle of low-lying huckleberry oak that grabbed my legs and pulled me backward whenever it could. Then in the open I strode up the rocky slope that became more and more severe, first scattered in large rocks and in plentiful smaller rocks, then with combinations of rocks of every size along with pitches where the rocks had been sorted by gravity into groups, each in its own remarkably uniform grade. Then the slopes curved up steeper and took me across snowfields where I kicked steps into the hardened crust that had begun to soften in the mid-morning sun. With each step, the view outward expanded. On the west side of the ridge, I could see a widening panorama of foothills. Crossing over to the east side, I saw that the rocky chaos of the Sierra's spine took on greater apparent order as I climbed higher and gained more of a bird's-eye view. I breathed harder in the thinning air, but stepped faster with increasing anticipation for the scene that awaited.

Before noon, I rested on top.

To the north, Mount Price and several other peaks rose much like Pyramid does, only smaller, and the Rubicon River flowed northwest toward its confluence with the Middle Fork American. Far beyond, the Sierra Nevada dropped off into lower forested country typical of the range's northern end.

To the east, Angora Peak and Mount Tallac pitched precipitously down toward the blue gem of Lake Tahoe. To the south, a sensational view reached sixty miles toward Sonora Peak. The sweep of mountain country appeared to be unlimited in its promise of beauty, adventure, and everything else that the Sierra might mean to me.

To the west the terrain dropped sharply for two thousand feet to the forest belt of the Sierra, incised by a curving network of canyons that eventually ran together like branches running down the length of a tree to the larger trunk of the American River. Beyond, the yellow softness of the foothills continued to descend with slopes here and there darkened by chaparral and clusters of gray pine, and then to lighter-colored slopes that I knew were oaks scattered in grass. Below that, the haze of urban and agricultural California took over completely and obscured the tentacles of sprawl that follow the corridor of Highway 50 up to Placerville and Interstate 80 up to Auburn. On a clear day—perhaps in winter and on a weekend, when people don't drive as much—I would easily have seen the entire city of Sacramento and the coastal mountains beyond. But now my distant view revealed only the double-toothed summit of Diablo, the highest peak in the Coast Range east of San Francisco. I could see only its very top, faintly visible above the sea of smog.

All at once, the great paradox of the Sierra Nevada was apparent to me just by looking around. The mountains lay in wild, rugged splendor, spotted with shining lakes, incised by raging rivers, blanketed by the deep green refuge of forests. But just beyond, the extent and the effects of urban California were bluntly evident in the air it produced—gray enough, yellow enough, thick enough to completely obscure everything beneath it. Here on the summit of Pyramid, both wilderness and its antithesis could be seen in one eyeful. I could tell that a large part of the Sierra experience would forever be a matter of coming to terms with that strange, troubling, and fateful paradox.

When I was listening to the music of the stream down below, I had wondered what else I might hear on Pyramid beyond the whistling of wind and the clatter of falling rocks. Now, with only a modest engagement of my imagination, I could hear the mountains calling me onward, upward, inward.

Pyramid offered a good introduction to the greater mountain world. Thousands of other peaks rise in this range, and as I clearly saw from this first rocky summit, the mountains are cloaked in forests on all but the highest and most rugged slopes. A savanna of oaks decorates the lower western reaches, and through it all, rivers run down from the highest passes to the deepest canyons like lifelines to all of the land around them.

With anticipation that had been building for miles as I approached the snowy crown of the pass, I gazed out across the headwaters of the Kings River. In several loosely linked trips, I planned to follow the water's route downstream in order to see this river from its beginning to its lower elevations, where it leaves the Sierra Nevada.

At the base of Muir Pass, 11,600 feet above sea level in Kings Canyon National Park, the Middle Fork of the Kings takes shape with glistening meltwater trickling from snowbanks, still deep even in midsummer. From there to the backwater of the uppermost reservoir at 950 feet above sea level, this river has the greatest undammed vertical drop of all the rivers of America. (Higher mountains in Alaska are blanketed in glaciers, some extending down to sea level; all obscure any high-elevation rivers that might lie beneath the ice.) The route of the Kings would also take me through America's deepest canyon—nearly 3,000 feet deeper than the Grand Canyon of the Colorado and also deeper than Hells Canyon of the Snake River.

Up there at the beginning, Sierra Nevada peaks rise skyward as the river adds small tributaries and begins its remarkable descent by foaming through the granite-walled wildness of LeConte Canyon. The splashing volume of Palisade Creek, nourished all summer long by the melting of glaciers, joins from the east. From there I hiked for two days and sixteen miles, past dozens of white-water chutes and green pools of unknown depth. I camped in clusters of lodgepole pines edging bright meadows and in flickering sunlight within yellow-green groves of cottonwoods.

The river then entered Tehipite Valley. Rock-clad, cliff-sided, this short respite in the river's tumultuous course lies beneath Tehipite Dome, a 3,600-foot-tall shaft of granite—the thinnest high dome of granite I've ever seen. From there, the only trail climbs in dozens of switchbacks out of the canyon, leaving the lower cascades of the Middle Fork inaccessible. I hiked out on a complicated maze of trails eventually leading me to the top of Spanish Mountain, where the river, 8,240 vertical feet below, is not even visible.

The main stem of the Kings forms where the Middle Fork is joined by the South Fork, which has followed an equally impressive path down from the high Sierra at Mather Pass and through a popular recreation area called Cedar Grove. With more power in its combined flow, the Kings then courses through drier but no less spectacular canyons. Tributary waterfalls splash directly into the riverbed. Gardens of indigestible boulders choke the channel. Rugged trails reach the river at only a few places, such as Yucca Point—my next trailhead, found along the winding road to Cedar Grove.

This rocky path took me quickly to the river, but from there I could walk up- or downstream only short distances before being confronted with vertical cliffs. Other than going back, the only option was to swim across the river. Leaving my camera behind, I did this a couple of times on the hot summer day, but I didn't get much farther before

Kings River below Mill Flat Creek
This excellent trout fishery and white-water stream was protected in 1987 when the Committee to Save the Kings River stopped an unnecessary dam from being built here below Mill Flat Creek.

the swimming and the rocks all became increasingly difficult, my means of returning in doubt.

The gradient eases eight miles downstream at Garnet Dike, reachable by dirt road. Here the tight-walled gorge opens slightly to the Sierra foothills. Nine miles later, with its breathtaking, free-flowing drop of 10,650 vertical feet completed, the Kings pools into Pine Flat Reservoir in the lower foothills.

Though extraordinary by any measure, the Kings also typifies other rivers of the Sierra and clearly shows the importance of the waters' flow everywhere.

Seismic forces build the mountains up to the high peaks and ridges, and then erosion by rivers such as the Kings wears them down; the Sierra is still in the process of being formed. Water erodes ravines, canyons, and valleys, pushing rock, sand, and silt forcibly downstream, sometimes just one stone-turn at a time, sometimes in a slow-motion avalanche of rocks clacking against other underwater rocks during the height of a flood.

Water is a powerful shaper of canyons in its liquid form but even more potent as ice. The highly abrasive force of glaciers has scoured the range in supremely artful ways throughout the high and middle elevations. Glaciers have scraped out U-shaped canyons at the upper reaches of streams and torn large bites from mountain faces by their perennial freezing and thawing at every interface with rock. Mounds of boulders, gravel, and grit were pushed by the leading blade of the bulldozing glaciers and stacked high in moraines that still mark the exact spot where the glaciers peaked and then began to recede. Nearly all of the Sierra's four thousand lakes resulted from glacial excavations. The ongoing work of ice can still be seen on the North Palisade and other peaks that ring the headwaters of the Kings River, and at sixty glaciers on north faces throughout the highest Sierra, though the ice is now receding rapidly in the age of global warming. Year by year, entire glaciers will disappear.

Virtually all the stellar scenery that we know in the Sierra today was shaped by water in either its liquid or solid form. A Sierra Nevada with minimal rain and snow would look a lot like the White Mountains,

to the east, which rise nearly as high but lie in the rainshadow of the Sierra, and so they experience far less erosive washing through wet storms, gouging glaciers, and the relentless work of rivers.

Photographing the Sierra constantly reminds me of the vitality and importance of water. Even when I'm far away from the riffles of streams or the reflections of lakes, what I see is determined by the rock that has been taken away by water; the negative space is just as important as the positive. The valley of Yosemite, the canyon of the Kings, the low dip of each mountain pass—all of them owe their shapes to what was subtracted by the runoff of rain and snow.

If there's anything as fundamental as the shape of the earth's surface, it's the ability of that earth to support life, and for this, water is likewise essential. Virtually everything that lives needs water, and in the Sierra's Mediterranean climate of wet winters and dry, sun-baked summers, much of the community of life congregates at the streams. Up to 70 percent of bird and wildlife species depend on habitat along the water at some point in their lives, if not every day. The riparian, or riverfront, zones rank as the most crucial among all landscapes for the health of biological communities and whole ecosystems.

Furthermore, water is beautiful, and when I roam the mountains with my camera, I never fail to be stopped by the flow. There's always something elegant about this simple, common substance—so extraordinary when combined with the Sierra's gradient and the Sierra's luminous light. Shimmering, riffling, bubbling, reflecting, constantly moving, water catches my eye and holds it.

Perhaps some of my enchantment with the flow stems from this fact: our bodies are more than two-thirds water. If we didn't drink, we could die in three days. For most of us, that water comes from rivers and springs. The streams literally flow in our veins, and I always feel closer to this truth when I arrive at high, remote destinations in the Sierra, dip my hands in the fresh snowmelt, and drink.

Among all the waterways in America, not only the Kings but other Sierra rivers are exceptional for their steep gradient and purity, at least in the higher reaches. The clarity owes to wildness. Here we find few roads and little development, which both cause siltation elsewhere.

SOUTH FORK AMERICAN RIVER
From the Feather River in the north to the Kern River in the south, streams carry the abundant snowmelt of the Sierra down steep mountain slopes. The South Fork of the American riffles among alders downstream from Coloma.

In addition, Sierra watersheds are largely composed of granite, which produces little silt or mud.

At high elevations, Sierra rivers are a showcase of tumbling mountain water. At middle elevations, Sierra rivers course past hanging valleys. These are where main-stem glaciers excavated so much of the valley soil and rock that they left tributary streams "hanging" up above. These became the sites of waterfalls, which many people regard as the supreme highlights of Sierra scenery. At low elevations, the Sierra rivers burst through foothill canyons, bringing nourishment to an increasingly hot land. Rivers at this elevation also draw people by the thousands to enjoy the excitement of white-water paddling.

I had seen the upper and middle elevations of the Kings on foot, and now, not just at the river, but *on* it, I was learning more than I had ever

expected to know about the force of water. In a grand finale to my Kings River explorations, I suddenly found myself entering Rooster Tail Rapid. The current accelerated, the channel narrowed, the edges mounded up in diagonal waves that funneled me toward a vortex hidden by a crest of foam that preceded whatever might follow. I couldn't tell what lay ahead, and the unknown can be a frightening thing.

Thus far, canoeing on the Kings below Garnet Dike had been a pleasure. The day was full of beauty and fun in the way that only a day on a river can be. Perfect.

As the snowmelt had waned in the preceding weeks, the river level had dropped. The Kings took on a transparent clarity, its pools like reflecting basins with surfaces as green and shiny as mint jelly, its rapids like crisp white stairsteps of foam. Now I paddled along with a group of friends who guided rafts for an outfitting company called

Zephyr. Piloting their larger, stable craft, they said they would rescue me if I needed help, and with a trust that comes from outdoor partnerships of this type, I knew that they would.

The first rapid, called Bonsai, had me scrambling to miss some boat-eating holes where the current swirled deep and then rebounded with heart-thumping waves that made rafting a challenge and canoeing a bona fide struggle.

Following that stormy entrance, the river curved with watery charm. Colored cobbles shimmered down deep, willows and sycamores greened shorelines alive with birds, and valley oaks boldly towered above the banks. Though they grow on the higher benches, these giant trees are no less dependent than willows on the quenching flow of the river; they tap its moisture with roots that probe forty feet down to where groundwater is replenished by the seasonal flooding of the Kings.

Above the oaks, smooth sweeps of grass waved in the breeze on slopes too steep for walking, and above that, the grass gave way to multiple textures of thick, unshaven, unpenetrable chaparral. Above it I saw spiked groves of ponderosa pines, and finally, at the top, the wide-reaching, upright limbs of sugar pines and a shaggy dark forest of fir that serrated the ridgelines like the teeth of a comb.

Down where my Zephyr friends and I boated, the Kings flourished in one final accumulation of power and glory before it pooled into a twenty-mile-long reservoir and then eased out across the southern Central Valley. Down there, irrigation companies have subdivided the flow into large canals, then smaller canals, large ditches, then smaller ditches, and on and on until nothing, absolutely nothing is left.

In my canoe I occasionally eddied out to bail water and to soak up the scenery during placid reprieves from the linked chain of rapids. Halfway through the trip, I beached with the fleet of rafts at Mill Flat Creek, where we swam in sun-warmed pools that lent a tropical feel to the day. We lingered over a savory lunch and lounged in shade, sat in the water, re-warmed in the sun, and finally waded back into the river and boarded our boats when it was time to go.

In 1891 John Muir proposed a national park for this reach of the Kings, all the way down to Mill Flat Creek, but his vision for the Sierra was only partly realized when, years later, Congress established Kings Canyon National Park upstream. Seeing the Kings with different eyes, an organization of farmers and agribusinessmen proposed that a dam be built at Rogers Crossing—just below Mill Flat Creek—in 1985. Cheaper alternatives were available for irrigation water, which wasn't even needed for the basin's heavily subsidized crops; the water might have been sold for urban use elsewhere. The dam would have eliminated the finest trout fishery of its size in California, one of the best white water rafting runs, and a valley of unmatched beauty, with its savanna of burly oaks and sycamores, its remote refuge of fishing holes, and its choice habitat for wintering deer and whole communities of wild creatures.

The Committee to Save the Kings River defeated the dam proposal and saved the river with congressional legislation in 1987, and I worked for them on the campaign. For now, the stream and its life are protected. But nothing is secure forever. People who value the Kings may have to fight for its safety once again, and then again, as long as the population of California continues to grow.

Floating in my canoe down below the site that had been proposed for damming, my immediate concern was not for the river's future but for my own as I now stared into the mysterious maelstrom of Rooster Tail Rapid. Over the eons, the river had inevitably had its way with the mountains, carving the canyon and pushing suspended soil down to fill the geologically depressed Central Valley with twenty thousand feet of sediment. In a far shorter time frame, the river would have its way with me as well.

At that instant I was jetted up on a towering wave where I perched, for the briefest, wide-eyed snapshot of time, on top. A world of uncompromising wetness lay below, and I sensed, in a way I never had before, the total power of a river. Feeling its force underneath me, I knew perfectly well how it could win its age-old battles with rock. Each eroded canyon in the Sierra shows that the Irresistible Force indeed wins when pitted against the Immovable Object.

I never really had a chance.

I was dropped unceremoniously into the sudsing pit beyond the flamboyantly arched jet of flow that inspired raft guides to name this rapid after the tail of a rooster. The canoe filled with water as if a ten-foot swell at a steep ocean beach had slammed instantaneously over my bow. I felt my whole unit—body, boat, and soul—penetrate the river and enter its interior in a way that buoyant things are not supposed to do. I had enjoyed being *at* the river, and then *on* it, but now I was *in* it.

Miraculously I stayed in the canoe—my thighs wedged under straps that help to hold me secure—and I floated up out of the whiteness once again, completely englossed in water and still clutching my paddle as if I had another shot at life. But now at the mercy of hundreds of pounds of the Kings River filling my boat and sloshing back and forth, I lacked stability. The next wave knocked me over, forcing me to swim to shore, side-stroking while towing my boat in the wide protection of an eddy directly below the rapid. My Zephyr friends offered to help, but the big eddy marked the end of the trip, and Rooster Tail marked one final triumph for the river before it hit the slack water of the reservoir just around the next bend.

I had drunk at the source of the river, explored its great canyons, revered its sculptural artwork at Tehipite, and basked in the pleasures of placid pools and swift deliverance. With my total immersion in the river's final rapid, my tour of the Kings was complete, and I felt an inseparable bond to this magnificent stream like I had never felt before.

Like the Kings, each of the Sierra's rivers occupies its own distinguished place in the geography of the range. Twelve major streams and several minor ones carry the winter rainfall of the foothills and the snowmelt of the high mountains westward toward San Francisco Bay or to land-locked sinks of the southern San Joaquin Valley, and four others run toward the Great Basin. Like the peaks whose runoff they carry, each

river is an exemplar of mountain life, each with its own specialties and beauty.

At the northern boundary of the range, the Feather cuts westward, nearly twice the size of the next largest river in the Sierra. The North Fork is so heavily dammed, piped, and diverted for hydroelectric power

TUOLUMNE RIVER ABOVE BIG CREEK
Deceptively calm, the Tuolumne above Big Creek gathers strength for another tumultuous rapid in one of the West's finest white-water runs, which extends for eighteen miles, from Meral's Pool to Ward's Ferry. The Tuolumne River Trust and Friends of the River halted plans to divert the river's flow near here by persuading Congress to include its upper reaches in the National Wild and Scenic Rivers system, which bans dams, diversions, and harmful developments.

that, for now, one might think of it more as plumbing than geography. In contrast, much of the Middle Fork remains wild until it hits the backwater of Oroville Dam, tallest in America at 770 feet. The Middle Fork was among America's first twelve rivers to be designated in the National Wild and Scenic Rivers system, which protects against further damming or development on federal land near the waterfront.

The next river southward is the North Yuba, flowing steep and shadowy in dark forests. Power companies have tapped the South Yuba heavily, yet an exquisite reach remains, now protected in the California State Scenic Rivers system thanks to the work of the South Yuba River Citizens League.

The North Fork American rumbles in deep canyons with names such as Royal Gorge and Giant Gap. Along the South Fork of the American, the California Gold Rush began when one big nugget was found at Coloma. Both above and below that site, the South Fork has become the most floated whitewater in the West.

MERCED RIVER
One of the finest rivers of the Sierra, the Merced winds through the sublime Yosemite Valley and then drops into a rugged granite canyon.

South of there, the small Cosumnes is the only river flowing the whole way to sea level without a major dam. Bordering its basin, the Mokelumne begins near the Sierra crest and tears through a wild canyon before encountering the usual spate of lower-elevation dams.

The Stanislaus' North Fork penetrates a stunning showcase of forest and rock. The Middle Fork emanates from the high open peaks of Sonora Pass, and the South Fork from the granite expanse of the Emigrant Wilderness. Once the West's most popular whitewater, the main-stem Stanislaus was flooded by New Melones Dam in 1980.

Deep in the lore of conservationists and river runners, the Tuolumne draws headwaters from northern Yosemite National Park, drops through its own Grand Canyon, pools into a reservoir at Hetch Hetchy Valley, and then breaks free for one more wilderness beloved by white-water boaters and trout anglers.

The Merced plunges over spectacular drops and then collects tributaries that ring Yosemite Valley with the most remarkable set of waterfalls in America. Then the river pushes through a rugged canyon to the foothills.

Some millennia ago the seismic rise of the Sierra crest truncated the headwaters of the San Joaquin River, and the stream still nearly penetrates the entire width of the range west of Mammoth. Wilderness areas surround a remote midsection decorated with domes of granite before it encounters the dams and diversions that ultimately suck this lifeline of the middle Sierra dry.

The Kings is the next river to the south, followed by the Kaweah, which draws from the high granite of Sequoia National Park. Finally, the southwestern limits of the range are the home of the Kern River. Flowing from the western flanks of Mount Whitney, the North Fork cuts an earthquake-cleft canyon so straight it appears to have been lined up with a ruler. Below Isabella Reservoir, the main stem pours through boulder-jammed rapids before encountering canal headgates that divert every drop to industrial-scale farming operations.

With smaller but no less striking rivers, the eastern Sierra drains into the Great Basin—a region that extends across Nevada. The rivers there are landlocked, lacking access to the sea, and so end in lakes or irrigation ditches.

The Truckee first fills the emerald vastness of Lake Tahoe. With a depth of 1,685 feet, it's America's second-deepest lake and holds more water than all the other lakes and reservoirs in California combined. After bisecting the city of Reno, the Truckee ends in Nevada's Pyramid Lake. To the south, the Carson gathers its West Fork from the fine meadowlands of Hope Valley. The East Fork flows wildly in a north-bound route within the Sierra and then cuts eastward through sage-covered hills. The Walker River crashes off the escarpment near Sonora Pass. Farther southward, the magnificent landlocked gem of Mono Lake collects six small streams. The remainder of the Sierra's east-side runoff gravitates toward the Owens River, which Los Angeles dries up by piping it to the city.

The mountains owe their shape and life to all these rivers, but the rivers would not exist at all without the mountains. The Sierra massif is what forces the clouds to rise higher, which causes the air to cool and the water vapor to condense and then fall as rain and snow.

The winter storms are what make the rivers run, and the thick mantle of snow that blankets the high Sierra from November to June determines how life will be lived in the mountains.

At no time have I felt closer to the center of mountain power than during a snowstorm in the Sierra.

Dressed for the day, I set out from the cabin where I spent one winter at Horseshoe Bend, near Donner Pass. The low, gray ripples in the sky and a breath of moist air told me that a storm was on the way.

The icy, early morning snow crunched under my skis. A crystalline veneer had frozen into cement-like hardness through a whole week of mostly sunny weather that repeatedly thawed the outer skin of the snowpack by midday, only to have crisp nights refreeze it again after dark. Each cycle of thaw-and-freeze hardened the accumulation further, decreasing its depth, increasing its density, adding to the water content of each inch that remained.

This kind of snow made for horrible skiing—it was difficult to turn on a surface that ski edges could not cut. Even with climbing skins on the bottoms of my skis, which provided traction, the steep slopes on uphill climbs had a cunning slipperiness to them. Still worse, as I glided downhill, the glazed crust once in a while broke with no predictability except for always happening at the worst possible time, burying one ski or the other and sometimes causing me to fall. Being alone, I took no chances and avoided even moderate downhill runs in such poor conditions. But I kept going, counting on the weather and the snow conditions to change.

I paused to reconsider my route once I reached the top of a familiar saddle where rounded slopes rose to my left and right. Mountain junipers and Jeffrey pines lay scattered in the snowbound granite, and I watched the incoming waves of clouds darken the western sky. Sections of the background began to blur and then fade from sight beneath the thickening blue-gray atmosphere. The snow out there had begun to fall, and I knew that it would begin to fall on me, as well, in a matter of minutes. I smiled at the possibility, because I realized that to truly know these mountains, one must know the nature of snow.

The Sierra was even named for its snow. In 1776 Pedro Font wrote that he saw "una gran sierra nevada"—a great snow-covered range (from this etymology, "Sierra" is a "range" and is properly singular, not plural). The Franciscan missionary was simply describing what he saw from a distance, but the name stuck, perhaps because it caught the essence of the place as well as any single phrase could do.

Jutting skyward to a crest from 6,000 to 14,000 feet, and running continuously without any low breaks in a north-northwest to south-southeast direction, the Sierra forms an effective obstacle to the eastward drifting clouds, and the amount of water thereby gleaned from them is extreme. On the Ebbetts Pass road, a record of thirty-two and a half feet of snow accumulated in a single month. In the United States, only the Cascades, the Olympic Mountains, and the Coast Ranges of Alaska receive heavier snowfall. Except for losses to sublimation when the snow evaporates directly back into the

SOUTH YUBA RIVER
A winter storm at Donner Pass nearly buries the South Yuba River in snow. Red fir, mountain hemlock, whitebark pine, and lodgepole pine all thrive at the Sierra's snow-covered elevations.

atmosphere, the white frosting remains until the spring or summer, when melt-off recharges the rivers.

With its white mantle lasting eight months a year, winter is the long season in the high country. The grip of cold and the depth of snow determine what will grow and live there, when we can travel there, and what we will see when we arrive.

Fresh snow piled on top of a packed base makes for excellent skiing, but when the new snow arrives, avalanche hazards increase because the light new snow has no way to bond with the hardened crust beneath. Slides can strike with unimaginable force, sounding like underground freight trains, shearing off trees at head-height, engulfing everything in their paths. Most people buried in large avalanches die.

CARSON PASS
On a blustery winter day, a skier traverses Elephant's Back, south of Carson Pass.

The tumbling snow creates friction, which even on cold days melts some of the snow and yields a heavy, lumpy batter. This immediately refreezes as soon as the snow stops moving. The entire pile of debris then instantly sets up like mortar—the proverbial cement boots, only in this case a whole cement body bag. Victims cannot move, let alone dig themselves out.

Highly averse to this kind of death, I avoid all the avalanche slopes I can identify.

Looking forward to the softness and the traction of the new snow but not to the hazards, I welcomed the first flurries that began to fall. Big white flakes soon speckled the atmosphere as far as I could see and landed on my jacket like the artistic masterpieces they were, some pointed and glistening in the shape of diamonds, some like stars. Some melted against my face and ran down my neck. If I stayed out in the storm, I would get wet by small but cumulative increments, owing to melted snowflakes, sweat, and condensation of my body moisture against the inside of my storm parka. If I became stranded—by getting lost, for example, or hurt—this wetness could spell a greater hazard than the most violent of avalanches.

The wind can howl when it snows. In fact, that very storm worked up to a sandblaster's intensity the next day, but there at the start, the snow fell in big airy flakes that drifted down by wavering routes from the clouds and, in complete silence, accumulated deeper, deeper, deeper. Far from generating alarm about the dangers of winter, the silence and the continuous, regular drop of the snowflakes relax me with a nearly hypnotic effect. When snow falls in that way, I love to simply stand and stare. Falling snow can mesmerize me in ways that even the magic of flowing water cannot do. Sometimes when I'm awake in the night and cannot go back to sleep, I imagine this Sierra scene of slowly, steadily dropping snowflakes in front of somber green fir trees, and I fade away in comfort.

Within an hour of the flurries' onset, an inch of new snow covered the ground and outlined every branch, every tree trunk, every thin line of every needle on the pines as though the whole world had suddenly been painted anew. In another hour three inches covered the ground,

and what had been thin lines of new snow on the branches became bulky white masses of it. The pileup buried my ski tracks almost as fast as I made them.

Visibility dropped to a few hundred feet, and without any of the usual landmarks in sight, I made sure that I remembered my route—directly south along a gently sloped ridgetop. I kept it simple and avoided the kind of free-form traveling that always tempts me in the Sierra's big open spaces. I also watched my compass to make sure I didn't steer off in the arcing curve of lost people who walk in circles because either their left or right stride is consistently longer than the other one. Unlike wandering off course in summertime, which has relatively carefree consequences, getting lost in the winter can be life-threatening in a matter of no time. I adhered to a straight line by repeatedly eyeing two trees—one near and one far—and skiing directly between them.

Trees take on remarkably different personalities in a deepening storm. All of them must cope with the snow, which by the end of winter can reach compacted depths of twelve feet. The mountain hemlocks meet this challenge by bending, which allows fresh snow to slide off the foliage and drop onto the ground around the trees, where it adds to the roots' future water supply. Making a virtue of suppleness and flexibility, the hemlock limbs spring back up after disposing of their load. With a completely different strategy, red fir trees are pointed, and hold their shape, and when they are covered by snow, the ghostlike trees begin to shed further accumulations the way a steep roof does. Mountain junipers lack the obelisk shape of the firs and respond to the snow with brute force. Stiff and strong, their branches withstand even the heavy weight of wet snow, freezing rain, and ice. Lodgepole pines appear less capable, yet in the snow zone they are often the most plentiful tree. They sag under heavy loads, and young pines sometimes bend completely over. Few of them, however, are brittle enough to break. Some become permanently deformed by winters spent pinned in unflattering positions beneath the weight of snow, but they continue to grow, sometimes in such strangely contorted shapes that they have been harvested for use as an architectural art form.

By the hour, all these strategies for survival were becoming more evident, and I knew that I had to consider my own strategy as well. Visibility had decreased yet another notch, and gusts of wind had begun. I decided enough was enough, and returned to my cabin by noon. There I enjoyed the intensifying show from a south-facing window. Snow piled higher and higher on my deck. I stoked a wood stove with cured lodgepole pine—the best firewood above the zone of oaks—and heated water for tea.

My cabin was reasonably airtight and secure, but the storm seemed to blow its growing energy right through the walls, and the excitement of its power was palpable. The wind began to gust and channel snow into drifts that soon buried whole logs and boulders and altered the entire lay of the land. The few birds and mammals that weather winter at high elevations—gray-crowned rosy finches, chickadees, and snowshoe hares—all hid, a sure sign of a serious storm under way.

Much as my first view of the Sierra in Lee Vining Canyon had whetted my appetite for more of the mountains, my short skiing outings in the northern Sierra sparked a desire to see more of the long season. As the snow piled up higher all around me, I got out my maps and planned an expedition to a place where I could appreciate both the beauty and bite of winter in the high country. But to gain an important survival advantage, I would wait until the longer days when winter begins to turn into spring.

With my pack loaded full of gear and food for five days, and an avalanche shovel strapped on back, I began skiing where the caterpillar-tracked snowplow had been forced to quit on the road to Lake Sabrina, west of Bishop. I followed the interred road until it ended, and then I was on my own, all trails deep out of sight.

Using stream courses, valleys, ridges, and identifiable summits as monuments marking my course, I navigated toward Piute Pass, on the Sierra crest. Months before, snow had buried the trail, but it had also covered the rocks, shrubs, and fallen timber that can make cross-country travel maddeningly difficult during summer. In mid-April, all

MOUNTAIN JUNIPER
Fresh snow on a wind-free day piles up around this mountain juniper, which may have survived a thousand winters at its spare and exposed site near Carson Pass.

those obstacles lay beneath the smooth frosting of winter, still six feet deep.

In the warm sun of each April afternoon, an inch or two of snow on the top softened into coarse crystals known as "corn," ideal for skiing because it provides traction. Yet the underbelly of the snowpack remained rock-solid, with little danger of my breaking through. Likewise, the chance of an avalanche was minimal because the whole winter's accumulation had frozen and then melted and then refrozen so many times that it had bonded together, a welded mass that would remain stable until hot days arrived. Then the whole winter's mix would heat enough to cause heavy slides of wicked slush, some of it shearing off at ground level, crumbling, tumbling, and crushing everything in its avalanche path.

I avoided steep downhill slopes that could throw me off balance with the heavy pack. For several hours I worked my way up a valley sheltered by peaks north and south. Allowing time before darkness fell, I shoveled out a wind-sheltered slot for my tent in the lee of a granite boulder, fired up dinner on my tiny stove, melted some snow for a water bottle that I would take to bed with me, and zipped into my sleeping bag while the sun set and the temperature plummeted.

The next morning, coyote tracks ten feet from my tent showed where the wily dogs had come on their incessant roamings for mice and other prey, which still scurried beneath the snow and around wells that had melted at the base of trees. Being russet, gray, or almost black, tree trunks heat up in the sun and melt the snow immediately around them, providing some limited access to the ground.

After breaking camp, I skied onward toward Piute Pass. Breaking out of the last lodgepole pine forest, I traversed open meadows, a frozen lake that groaned with pressure changes as I crossed, and steepening slopes that angled in a concave profile to a pitch where granite outcrops knifed up so steeply that they had shed snow all winter long. In the bright morning sun, those ledges now dripped with meltwater. Avoiding the unstable wet snow near the rocks, I clung to safer slopes and soon emerged on top of the rise, relieved and panting in the thinning air at 10,000 feet.

A long swishing glide across higher meadows took me to the final pitch and the Sierra crest with its stunning westward view, a topography as grand as anything I had ever seen. Peaks jutted up and ridges rose like the great mountain walls they were. Outcrops of granite, sharp and angular, glistened like incisors, molars, buckteeth, and fangs. The soft uniformity of white covered everything else except scattered clusters of whitebark pines.

Muriel Peak towered to the south, a colossal monolith of rock and snow that cast long blue shadows over frozen lakes. Its buttresses linked with other summits and a continuous forbidding ridge called the Glacier Divide, which separates the sublime Evolution Valley to the south from the Piute Creek watershed to the north. Directly below in my view, Humphreys Basin invited me into its gentle swales and recesses, a great, perched oval of Arctic wilderness bounded on the east by the higher Sierra crest and on other sides by the dizzying rims of canyons whose walls plunge down to tributaries of the South Fork San Joaquin River.

With this tantalizing scene before me, I plotted a route for the next three days—a time of complete isolation from the outside world and complete surrender to the bonds of winter that hold the high country tight until the end of spring.

However, I didn't get to ski all the time. After a day of pleasant touring to the north, I set up my camp in the cover of a whitebark cluster near Pine Creek Pass and noticed an evening breeze beginning to rustle the tent. Through the night the wind increased steadily. In the morning, a bitter gale there at 11,000 feet blew loose snow in a ground storm that completely blurred the distinction between earth and air— a zone that now seemed neither solid nor gaseous.

Storms always get bad before they get worse, and so I thought I should probably ski down to a lower elevation for better shelter from whatever was still to come. But first I decided to check the conditions by going for a short spin around the tent.

Outside I immediately suffered debilitating whiteout. In this strangely disorienting experience, all perception of depth vanishes. The ground in front of me could have been three feet away or thirty,

I couldn't tell. It was all white. Without sunlight, there were no shadows. I saw no edges and no texture to tell me whether the next step was up, down, or flat. I could ski straight into an unexpected mound of drifted snow and fall on my face, or straight off an unexpected steep drop and fall on my back, never knowing which it was going to be.

Feeling almost seasick, and also knowing that avalanche threats had heightened to extreme levels at a time when I couldn't even see what lay around me, I pursued the only reasonable option and went straight back to the tent, which, fortunately, I was still able to see. I shook the new accumulation of drifting snow off the fly and returned to my sleeping bag for the rest of the morning.

The storm was more than I had bargained for in the month of April. Lying there, with nothing to do, I understood better the slow pace of winter, when other animals in the mountains spend days

MURIEL PEAK
The monolith of Muriel Peak rises at the Glacier Divide, east of Bishop.

and weeks simply waiting for the weather to change and for the welcome approach of spring. Mountain life teaches many things, including patience.

Though little of the transformation was yet under way, I knew that in the coming months the snowbanks would recede foot by foot, the green tips of grass and forbs would break through moist soil, the marigolds would bloom in sunny wet pockets, and the waters would swell in the rivers once again. The trails would reappear from beneath the snow, with opportunities for me to wander on them for days and weeks at a time.

The cycle of the seasons, along with the cycles of flowing water, of animal migrations, and of life-and-death-and-life-again would all become apparent as the snow melted and summertime returned to the Sierra Nevada.

SIERRA BUTTES
The Sierra Buttes, west of Yuba Pass, form
the range's northernmost craggy peaks.

MIDDLE FORK FEATHER RIVER
Among the first rivers in America to be protected in the National Wild and Scenic Rivers system,
the Middle Fork of the Feather drops into the resoundingly remote and rugged Bald Rock Canyon.
The Feather is the northernmost and by far the largest river in the Sierra Nevada.

OAK WOODLANDS AT SPENCEVILLE
A savanna of blue oaks and grassland stretches across the Spenceville Wildlife Management Area, west of Grass Valley. Developers proposed a massive subdivision in oak woodlands adjacent to this protected area.

43

CALIFORNIA BLACK OAK, SOUTH FORK AMERICAN RIVER CANYON NEAR COLOMA
Throughout the western Sierra, rivers cut steep canyons through the foothills.

44   SOUTH YUBA RIVER NEAR NEVADA CITY

The South Yuba River has sculpted granite into bowls and rocky artwork above Purdon Crossing, near Nevada City.
Though hydropower companies impounded and diverted the river at its headwaters, the South Yuba River Citizens
League prevented further damming of this popular stream through State Scenic River legislation in 1999.

CANYON LIVE OAK AND SOUTH YUBA RIVER
A canyon live oak grips rocky soil of the South Yuba Canyon above Edwards Crossing.

45

RICHARDSON LAKE, WEST OF LAKE TAHOE
Lodgepole pines and white firs reflect in the glassy
surface of this lake just north of Desolation Wilderness.

GRANITE CHIEF FROM ANDERSON PEAK
Winter snows linger into July on the ridge
running west from Granite Chief, at the
head of Squaw Valley.

JEFFREY PINES NEAR DONNER PASS
Twilight falls on a forest of Jeffrey pines, common on the east side of the Sierra and in some sites west of the crest, such as here at Hampshire Rocks.

CHAPARRAL IN THE SOUTH FORK AMERICAN RIVER CANYON
Black locust and other low-growing chaparral plants remain green into the autumn on shaded slopes of the South Fork American canyon near Coloma, where the discovery that initiated the Gold Rush was made.

DESOLATION WILDERNESS AND MIDDLE VELMA LAKE
Middle Velma Lake lies in the heart of Desolation Wilderness, one of the northern Sierra's most popular areas among hikers and backpackers.

FREMONT COTTONWOOD, SOUTH FORK AMERICAN RIVER
Autumn's shower of Fremont cottonwood leaves decorates the ground
along the South Fork of the American at Camp Lotus, near Coloma.

LAKE TAHOE AT SECRET HARBOR

At Lake Tahoe State Park, granite boulders make stepping-stones in the blue depths. Elsewhere in this heavily urbanized basin of the Sierra, erosion resulting from land development and air pollution from cars cause nitrogen to build up in the water. The resulting growth of algae will gradually transform Tahoe from blue to green unless the problems are corrected.

Hope Valley

Jeffrey pines, white firs, and aspens border a meadow in Hope Valley, at the eastern base of Carson Pass, south of Lake Tahoe. Once threatened by subdivision, high-tension power lines, and damming, the elegant valley has been protected as open space.

GROUND STORM WEST OF CARSON PASS
A ground storm of blowing and sometimes blinding snow creates
deep drifts and dangerous overhanging cornices on high ridgelines.
Forbidding winds blast the summit of Round Top in the background.

BUCKWHEAT AT CARSON PASS

Buckwheat brightens a sagebrush-covered slope on the
east side of Carson Pass. About fifty species of this flower,
ranging from prostrate blooms to sizable shrubs, can be
found in the Sierra.

ELEPHANT'S BACK

When winds force hot summer air over the mountains in late afternoon,
thunderheads build at the Sierra crest near Carson Pass.

HAWKINS PEAK AND LIGHTNING STRIKE
Lightning generated by afternoon thunderstorms often strikes the Sierra peaks, especially those isolated from other high country, such as Hawkins Peak, above the West Fork of the Carson River.

MONITOR PASS

From an eastern arm of the Sierra called the Pine Nut Range, Monitor Pass offers
this springtime view west to Round Top Mountain—seen with a sharp summit from
this perspective—and to steep slopes that drain into the West Fork Carson River.

RAYMOND CREEK WATERFALL
Near its source north of Ebbetts
Pass, Raymond Creek sprays over
dark volcanic rock.

58

SMALL LAKE NEAR EBBETTS PASS
Ice on high-country lakes doesn't melt until June. A late-season snowstorm brews in the background.

INDIAN PAINTBRUSH
Twenty-one species of paintbrush bloom in the Sierra Nevada. Growing amid sage, this cluster brightens the scene along the Pacific Crest Trail near Raymond Peak.

EBBETTS PASS AND THE CARSON-ICEBERG WILDERNESS
The view from peaks above Ebbetts Pass shows deep snow lingering on
north-facing slopes. A small avalanche of heavy, wet snow has recently
broken off from the cornice appearing on the long ridgeline to the left.

Mountain juniper

Twisted and wind-blasted, this mountain juniper
clings to life in harsh terrain near the Sierra crest.

WESTERN WHITE PINES
The largest high-elevation trees in the northern Sierra, western white pines stand against a backdrop of volcanic rock warmed by evening light. Mountain junipers, Jeffrey pines, and red firs also find adequate pockets of soil on this flank of Reynolds Peak.

WHITEBARK PINES IN THE EMIGRANT WILDERNESS
At the very edge of timberline, some clusters of whitebark pines thicken while others weather into wind-blasted snags at the head of Kennedy Creek.

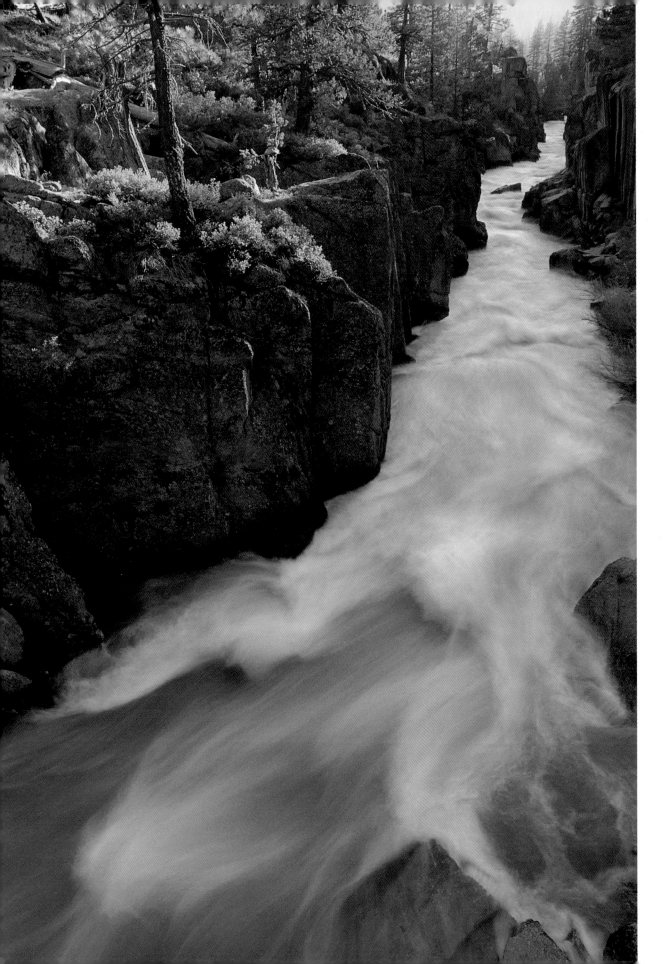

MIDDLE FORK STANISLAUS RIVER
Rushing with the snowmelt of Sonora
Pass, the Middle Fork Stanislaus carves
through a narrow gorge above Pigeon
Flat.

PACIFIC DOGWOOD AND NORTH FORK STANISLAUS RIVER

A harbinger of spring, Pacific dogwoods flower above the banks
of the North Fork Stanislaus near Sourgrass Bridge.

BLUE OAK AND FOOTHILLS NEAR THE STANISLAUS RIVER

A healthy oak spreads its limbs while new grass greens the springtime foothills in Skunk Gulch, above Parrotts Ferry. A year later, in 1980, this site was flooded by the backwaters of New Melones Dam.

66

LODGEPOLE PINES IN NORTHERN YOSEMITE NATIONAL PARK
East of Wilma Lake, huckleberry and azalea underlay lodgepole
pines at the edge of a reflective pond.

SMEDBERG LAKE OUTLET AND VOLUNTEER PEAK
To the west of Benson Pass, Volunteer Peak points skyward above a waterfall along the Pacific Crest Trail.

LYELL FORK, TUOLUMNE RIVER
With the Cathedral Range in the background, the Lyell Fork reflects the last light of the day and swishes through rapids, swirls into pools, and curls around small islands.

LODGEPOLE PINES AT SUNSET
Lodgepole pines cling to rocky slopes
above Tuolumne Meadows.

GRAND CANYON OF THE TUOLUMNE
A vein of white quartz stripes granite bedrock at
the rim of the Grand Canyon of the Tuolumne.

UNICORN PEAK AND THE TUOLUMNE RIVER
Thundering over its uppermost large waterfall, the
Tuolumne carries a flush of springtime runoff from
the Cathedral Range and other high-country locations.

WATERWHEEL FALLS
In the depths of its Grand Canyon,
the Tuolumne pounds downward in
a blizzard of early-summer runoff.

HALF DOME'S EASTERN FACE

At dawn, the moon sets behind the eastern face of Half Dome—
opposite from the mountain's better-known vertical wall seen
from Yosemite Valley. Cables, which aid hikers in climbing to the
summit, have been anchored onto the steep slope.

TENAYA CREEK
A new snowstorm has whitened the shorelines and forests of Tenaya Creek where it enters Yosemite Valley below Mirror Lake.

NEVADA FALL
The Merced River froths at the brink of 594-foot Nevada Fall—one of the most popular attractions in the backcountry of Yosemite National Park.

MERCED RIVER AND YOSEMITE VALLEY
In Yosemite Valley, granite cliffs rise from the
green riparian corridor of the Merced River.

YOSEMITE FALL IN WINTER
With two major pitches, Yosemite Fall drops nearly half a vertical mile into a valley blanketed by a recent snowstorm.

EL CAPITAN MEADOW
The Merced River drifts through Yosemite Valley and
nourishes a riparian corridor with springtime runoff.

CALIFORNIA GROUND SQUIRREL

A California ground squirrel investigates a promising morsel it has found on the forest floor of Yosemite Valley.

LODGEPOLE PINE CONES

Lodgepole pines grow throughout much of the Sierra's middle and high elevations and produce abundant crops of cones. Important to wildlife, the trees also burn intensely but germinate vigorously after fires; up to a hundred thousand seedlings can sprout per acre.

YOSEMITE FALL FROM TENAYA CANYON
Glistening in afternoon light, Yosemite
Creek free-falls 1,430 feet—creating one
of the tallest unobstructed waterfalls in
the world.

MERCED CANYON DOWNSTREAM FROM EL PORTAL
A blue oak unfurls new leaves while spring wildflowers
bloom. The searing heat of summer on the steep slopes
of the Merced Canyon will soon turn the oat-grass yellow.

ASPEN GROVE IN LUNDY CANYON, HOOVER WILDERNESS
Aspens congregate along Mill Creek, north of Lee Vining.
Chlorophyll in the bark gives the trunks a faintly green tint
and permits photosynthesis to occur even without leaves.
This enables aspen to survive in cold climates beyond the
range of most other deciduous trees.

ASPENS AT RUSH CREEK
A few rose hips—nutritious to wildlife—have ripened at the
base of this sun-drenched aspen grove along Rush Creek, an
important source of water for Mono Lake.

MONO LAKE AT SOUTH TUFA RESERVE

Eerie, beautifully surreal, and essential to millions of birds on their annual migrations, Mono Lake is a landmark at the northeastern edge of the Sierra. The cavitated rocks represent ancient accumulations of tufa—calcium carbonate deposited by water seeping from springs that the lake had covered in the past. Mono was in imminent danger of being reduced to a small fraction of its historic size because of diversions to Los Angeles. After a protracted battle, the Mono Lake Committee and other conservation groups prevailed. Renewed streamflows are now restoring the lake's water to an adequate level.

In Sequoia National Park the great tree rose three hundred feet into the violet-blue Sierra sky. The top disappeared from sight above the vivid green foliage of the crown. If I could count the hidden rings inside the bole, more than twenty feet in diameter, I might find several thousand. The sequoias are among the oldest living organisms on earth, surviving for up to thirty-five hundred years. The Sierra Nevada is a range of life, and these trees are as good a symbol for it as one might hope to find.

To get away from the cars and the crowds, I had walked a mile or so from the General Sherman Tree—the very largest. Alone now, and uninterrupted even by a whisper other than the springtime breeze, I sat silently at the base of the unnamed sequoia. I tried to think of the time it took to grow that much, and of all the winters and all the storms that the tree has endured. I tried to picture the view from the top, looking down so far on such puny creatures as we. Mainly, I delighted in simply being so close to a supremely successful living thing. It seemed large enough to have its own gravitational pull, and certainly did on my emotions. I admired the shape, the color, and the light as I futilely tried to capture the overwhelming essence of the tree in the lens of my camera.

The sequoias thrive in fertile soil at mid-elevations, 6,000 to 8,000 feet, where heavy winter precipitation soaks the ground and nourishes what John Muir called the greatest conifer forest in the world. In enclaves sheltered from glaciers during the last ice age, the giant trees survive at seventy-five distinct groves, from the Kern River basin in the south to the Middle Fork of the American.

Every plant and animal of the Sierra is uniquely adapted to the cycles of life there, and the sequoias offer a fascinating example of this because they live so long and grow so large.

On slopes sheltered by topography and by companionship with other sizable trees, such as sugar pines, the sequoias enjoy protection from the stiffest winds. Having roots that reach scarcely deeper than six to ten feet but can cover two full acres of ground, the trees need year-round moisture, so they grow in granite basins that catch and hold snowmelt. They also benefit from the moisture of summer thunderstorms, which coincidentally deliver the hazardous duo of lightning and fire. In a triumph of natural selection, the magnificent trees accommodate both.

The danger of fire is minimized by the trees' bark. Suffused with tannic acid, once a major ingredient in fire extinguishers, the russet-orange bark grows several feet thick—the elephant-skin of the plant world. The acid also repels insects, which plague other conifers in the driest summers but scarcely annoy the sequoias. Lower limbs of the trees die of their own accord and fall to the ground, preventing fire from advancing limb-to-limb upward and licking into the essential crown of foliage, which provides for the tree's substantial appetite through photosynthesis.

Not only do the sequoias protect themselves from fire; they need it. The cones open best when intensely heated, and the seeds then

GIANT SEQUOIAS IN GRANT GROVE, KINGS CANYON NATIONAL PARK
Quintessential symbols of life, giant sequoias are the largest trees in the world and among the oldest. These ancient trees have masterfully adapted to the Sierra and to its cycles of storms, moisture, parasites, lightning, and fire.

pop out unharmed. For successful germination and growth, the seeds require contact with mineral soil, which is exposed by fire. Furthermore, without recurrent fires to burn nearby white fir trees when they are small, those plentiful underlings would grow and create a fire-ladder whereby flames could climb up to the crowns of the sequoias and other large trees. The fire would then torch the entire forest rather than just creep along the ground.

Lightning itself poses no small hazard. Tall trees, after all, are among the best lightning rods on the planet, attracting the deadly jolts that seek the shortest distance between electricity-generating thunderheads and the grounding earth. But owing to the cellular structure of the sequoias' wood and to the way it physically conducts electrical charges through the fibers, the explosive shocks typically knock only cordwood-sized chunks off the top and fail to burn, splinter, or break the rest of the tree. Thus, the sequoias continue to get fatter as long as they live, but not taller, which would make them insupportable—top-heavy sails in the wind. Adapted in this

way, the trees take on their characteristic shape: their huge trunks terminate abruptly, without the typical steeple-like spike of many other conifers.

When the sequoias and other great trees of the Sierra die, they continue contributing to the ecosystem for hundreds and even thousands of years. Dead trees can actually support more life than live ones; insects, fungi, and microbes in unfathomable numbers tackle the necessary dirty work of decomposition. Young trees grow in the rotting remains of the old—a process as ancient as life and one that describes the ultimate cycle: the remains of the dead are absorbed by the living. Put another way, the individual dies but the system of life goes on.

Whether alive or dead, the trees emphatically do not grow in isolation. Deep forests of sequoia and other trees serve a wide assortment of creatures. Sierra forests are essential to the stealthy pine marten, the elusive fisher, and the endangered wolverine. Imperiled spotted owls need large trees with cavities that are formed when old snags rot. Eighteen vertebrate species depend on old-growth forests in the Sierra Nevada. Scores of others use the forests daily.

Woodpeckers, which eat tree-boring insects and thus keep outbreaks of beetles in check, need ancient forests. If the old cavity-ridden trees are eliminated, the birds' nesting sites disappear. With no woodpeckers, insect populations are more likely to explode, and otherwise healthy forests are ravaged by the bugs.

A healthy forest needs woodpeckers. Woodpeckers need old trees. Therefore, healthy forests need old trees and not just the fast-growing saplings or adolescent pole-timber of logged-over tracts—vital as these young forests might look in timber industry ads.

Forests illustrate how lives of many kinds are connected to each other, and also how all life is connected to the ruins and renewals of time. All over the Sierra, from the highest rock on Mount

JEFFREY PINE ALONG THE WEST WALKER RIVER
To overcome the hazards of a harsh environment and to scatter seeds for germination, Jeffrey pines produce plentiful crops of cones. Surplus seeds from many conifer species are important food for wildlife.

Whitney to the lowest tooth of granite in the foothills' final recline, the heartbeat of the mountains can be heard in the great cycles of life. These interlock with each other and set the stage for all the mountains' players to act out their individual lives.

On my very first walk in the Sierra, near Tioga Pass, I saw one of the noisiest of these players—a black-and-white Clark's nutcracker, which flew into thickets of whitebark pines. The bird orchestrates a cycle of life that I later discovered with fascination. First, I was not surprised to learn that the nutcrackers nest in the whitebarks and also eat the pine nuts—tasty seeds that they (and many people) extract from the cones. But I was intrigued to learn that the birds also carry seeds away in their beaks and bury up to fifteen at a time in the ground for later retrieval. A single bird can store up to thirty-eight thousand pine nuts a year—far too many to eat. Some of those conveniently planted seeds grow into new trees. Whitebark, limber, and bristlecone pines do not have winged seeds typical of other pines but rather depend on winged birds for seed dispersal. While the tree feeds the bird, the bird returns the favor by planting new trees, and the cycle of life goes on.

For some creatures, cycles of migration merge with the well-known cycles of seasons. I usually think of deer being at home wherever I see them. But in fact they follow long paths of migration every spring and fall, and the entire route constitutes their home. They spend summers in high terrain, where food grows plentifully owing to the lingering melt of snow and the water it provides. But like us, deer lack the ability to survive in bitter cold, and must come down to a reasonable elevation in the wintertime. For each drop of a thousand feet, the average temperature rises about three degrees. Conveying an unmistakable message to the deer, the blustery storms of November send whole herds of the graceful ungulates trotting down ridgelines toward the foothills. Successful hunters figure out where these ridgelines are, and then hope for snow.

Much like the deer, the rare bighorn sheep spend summer in the high country, but snow forces them down when it covers their food sources. The sheep remain at lower, but still wintry, windswept slopes until spring. Unlike deer, they avoid wooded tracts because the trees can conceal a mountain lion, whose life depends on the deer and sheep, and therefore on the ungulates' patterns of migration, and therefore on the health of continuous habitat all along the way.

Salmon begin life in streams of the Sierra, migrate out to the ocean for several years as adults, then migrate back up the rivers to spawn in streams that are relatively free of predators. This way they gain the protection of small streams when they are young and also access to greater food sources in the ocean when they are adults.

The salmon, bighorns, and deer show not only the importance of cycles in the life of the mountains, but also the importance of linkages—one habitat to another. Each of these species requires land at both high and low elevations, and the only way they can get from one to the other is by walking or swimming. To do this, they need corridors relatively uninterrupted by freeways, roads, dams, pollution, towns, suburbs, fences, cats, and dogs. It's not enough to protect a block of parkland, even the 748,000-acre Yosemite. The linkages to other reserves, to habitat at both high and low elevations, to water supplies, and to pathways along rivers are all important.

Fires burn in one of the most fascinating cycles, highly consequential to all the life in the forests. With the Pacific high-pressure weather system anchored off the California coast for at least six months a year, constantly pushing moist and low-pressure air away, the Sierra summers are dry and hot. Moisture evaporates, even from the surfaces of leaves, and this primes the forest for burning.

The intense summer heat also causes air masses over the heated ground to rise quickly, producing thunderstorms. These generate plentiful lightning, which ignites fires, but insufficient rain to put the fires out. Surprisingly, nature has thrived under these tough rules for eons. Human activity, however, has changed the condition of the forest dramatically in the past century and a half.

Before people began to put out the fires, much of the Sierra forest burned every seven to forty years, owing to lightning strikes. For millennia the Indians also set fires deliberately because burning augmented plants' production of nuts and berries, and it also enhanced the habitat for edible game, such as deer.

Far from becoming a charred wasteland, a forest of large trees thrived with frequent burning. The tall trunks of mature conifers held their crowns high above the reach of flames. Thick bark protected not only the sequoias but other large trees from serious damage.

The fires regularly burned fallen limbs, litter, and shrubs, leaving park-like groves of impressive trees with nutritious grasses and forbs underneath. Because the fires burned often, fuel on the ground did not accumulate, and so the fires seldom charred large areas but rather scorched spotty, curvilinear patterns, in what is called a fire mosaic. This allowed a wide mixture of tree species, sizes, and ages to coexist—all the better for wildlife. Nor did the frequent fires of the past usually burn hot enough to destroy microbes essential to the health of the soil.

Through thousands of years, many of the native plants adapted to these fire cycles, sprouting new shoots and greening up soon after burning. Some, such as the knobcone pine, actually required fire for their seeds to open. The ubiquitous lodgepole pine also needs fire. Furthermore, in the crackling dry summers of the Sierra, and even more in the semi-arid foothills, much of the dead plant debris failed to rot, and so the fires expedited the return of nutrients to the soil. With the nearly instantaneous breakdown of woody debris into ash, the critical building blocks of life became available to new plants in a way that would otherwise have taken years, if not centuries.

Wildlife, too, evolved with fire. Animals living under-ground survived by waiting for the flames to pass; they were mostly unaffected because the fires weren't lethal more than a few inches deep. Other animals evaded the flames—easy to do because the fires advanced in spotty patterns, rarely reaching catastrophic levels.

All this changed when people logged the old trees and prevented fires from burning in their ancient patterns. Lacking big trees, thickets of new growth germinated and grew without the pruning effect of frequent fire. The new forest lacked both the old-growth trees that resisted fire and the mosaic of burned and unburned areas—a pattern with many "breaks" that stop the progress of flames. Truly catastrophic fires are now common and growing worse. This can spell disaster to any homes that people build in harm's way, which means almost any home built in the Sierra Nevada.

We have so upset the natural balance between forest and fire that it's difficult to see how we will ever reinstate the healthy conditions that existed when John Muir wrote about sauntering easily through the park-like woodlands. Some scientists tell us to manually thin the thickets in order to recreate the mix of big trees and open understory, and then to allow frequent low-level fires to burn as they always did, even if this means setting the fires ourselves in carefully staged, controlled burns.

LUPINE ABOVE THE CHOWCHILLA RIVER
In springtime, the cycle of the seasons is evident with the blooming of lupine in the lower foothills northeast of Fresno.

WESTERN AZALEA NEAR BASS LAKE
In autumn, the shortening days prompt plants to prepare for winter. Western azaleas along Chilkoot Creek near Bass Lake turn from green to flaming orange and red. Wildlife readies for the long winter by storing food, migrating to lower elevations, or building fat reserves in the autumn and then hibernating.

Until large areas are restored, this solution explicitly excludes the logging of large trees. To withstand the encroachments of fire, a healthy forest needs large trees in order to limit the inflammatory undergrowth by shading it out, and to form breaks devoid of low-lying fuel. In these ways, stands of big trees interrupt or retard the advance of fires.

In one more cycle of nature in the Sierra Nevada, large predators hunt smaller species, to the ironic benefit of the smaller types of animals. Predators cull the weak and keep the numbers of prey within the carrying capacity of the food source. For example, without coyotes, ground squirrel and mouse populations can explode with myriad effects, including the denuding of grass on rangeland and the eradication of whole stands of new oak seedlings. Overpopulated colonies of rodents eventually become susceptible to disease, including bubonic plague, which can wipe out entire generations and affect other species, including people. Similarly, without mountain lions or wolves, deer numbers can increase until they over-eat the forest, eliminating young plant life up to a six-foot-high "browse line." This poses terminal problems to many important plant species, and also results in a sudden and catastrophic crash of the deer population once vegetation is grazed bare below the browse line.

All species in the Sierra ultimately depend on mountain slopes and gradients, on patterns of climate and weather, and on the interworkings of all other life forms around them. When we allow the cycles of life to operate, a healthy system results. Upsetting those cycles means not only undermining nature, but also risking the supply of fish and game that people eat or otherwise appreciate, the supply of water we drink, the growth of forests we harvest, the quality of air we breathe, and even the maintenance of climate that makes everything else possible.

My first trips to the Sierra Nevada were joyous outings, full of adventure and discovery. The quality of light, the clarity of air, the purity of water, the deep shade and resinous scent of the forest— all of it thrilled me and made me want to come back again and again. On each visit, I ventured to someplace new, and with each exploration my connection to the Sierra grew stronger. These mountains made me feel good, healthy, and happy, at once excited and peaceful.

Then I came to see the last days of the Stanislaus.

After I did, my life was forever changed.

Friends had told me that this secluded canyon of the Sierra foot-hills was about to be flooded, forever, by New Melones Dam. The river drew its runoff from high peaks and the Emigrant Wilderness. Its forks joined and then churned as a full-bodied stream through one of the deepest limestone canyons in the West, and paddlers enjoyed one of the premier white-water runs. My friends insisted that I see the place before it was too late, and I jumped at their urgent invitation.

I found a lush riparian corridor of willows, oaks, and cottonwoods. White sandy beaches invited campers to stop, relax, and enjoy the river's liveliness. Wildlife thrived along the water and fish jumped.

On flat slabs of bedrock we put our hands into bowl-like depressions that Miwok Indians had created by grinding acorns while they, too, had sat and watched the river running by, for the past ten thousand years.

But this was the last year.

The flow would soon end because the Army Corps of Engineers had built a dam downstream to prevent the winter flooding of pas-ture, crops, and mainly, costly orchards that had heedlessly been planted right up to the banks of the cyclically flooding river. Tragically, the Stanislaus was unnecessarily flooded and lost. Other means of reducing downstream flood damage were not only available but were more effective and economic—studies by state agencies proved this clinching point.

Unfortunately no one who cared about protecting wild places had even heard about the Stanislaus until a canoe-paddling biologist, Jerry Meral, went boating there and discovered what was at stake. Friends of the River organized and launched a spirited campaign, but the group never overcame the power of the dam supporters, who had big money at their disposal along with the advantage of an ingrained culture of water development married to unstoppable political momentum for halting the flow of the Stanislaus.

At the height of this campaign, I joined Friends of the River, and we did everything we could to stop the flooding. But ultimately we watched our river and all its life disappear under a morgue of advancing flat-water. Foot by excruciating foot, mile by agonizing mile, the reservoir buried all that we had known in that irreplaceable canyon—an Eden if there ever was one on earth.

While my first impressions of the Sierra had been formed in the wilds of the high country, seeing the loss of the Stanislaus opened my

STANISLAUS RIVER ABOVE PARROTTS FERRY
Flowing through a deep limestone canyon, the Stanislaus River was once the most-floated whitewater in the West and a scenic masterpiece. The extraordinary stream, including this site at Grapevine Gulch, was buried by New Melones Reservoir in 1980.

eyes to the changes occurring everywhere in the mountains. With the same tendency I have to look down with curiosity when I'm perched up on a peak, I now looked back up from my disappearing refuge along the lower Stanislaus, and I wondered how the rest of the range would bear the weight of the future as California's population grew.

Just as I had searched for beauty and adventure on my trips into the Sierra, I began to search for the less-welcome realities of our time. I wanted to know more than the joys of such a special place, more than the cycles of mountain life. I wanted to know what was really happening to the mountains, and I wanted to know why.

I began an uphill journey steeper than any climb I've ever done, but what I found must surely be important to anybody who cares about the Sierra.

I quickly learned that the Stanislaus was not the only threatened river. Water developers proposed other dams on some of the last free-flowing reaches of the South Yuba, the American, the Tuolumne, the Merced, the Kings, and the Kern. As it turned out, the unsuccessful campaign to save the Stanislaus marked a historic turning point that wasn't clearly evident at the time. But after 1982, any plan to destroy a wild river was met with effective opposition. The proposed dams on all those other rivers were stopped. However, on the American, the 685-foot-high Auburn Dam proposal has resurfaced repeatedly for thirty years and counting. The dam would flood up to fifty-eight miles of wild canyons. Earthquake hazards were discovered there only thirty miles upstream from Sacramento, causing the cost of the project to skyrocket. Though it has become emblematic of federal largesse and a mockery of sound water management, new incarnations of this risky multi-billion-dollar boondoggle keep resurfacing from congressmen otherwise claiming to be conservative.

Knowing about dam-related problems marked only the beginning of my search to understand the upcoming fate of the Sierra.

Though Lake Tahoe and its astonishing blue clarity have been the focus of the most concerted effort for clean water in America, the lake is increasingly clouded by algae. Far from natural, this is caused by silty runoff from land development and roadcuts, plus air pollution,

which causes nitrogen to accumulate in the lake. This important element properly resides in the air and soil and is taken up by plants that require it, but too much of that soil is now washing into the lake, where the nitrogen is taken up by algae. The cycle of nitrogen has been thoughtlessly misplaced—moved from land to water. Unless the trend can be halted, the bluest lake imaginable will turn into a green, slime-filled shadow of what we now know. The League to Save Lake Tahoe works to reverse this trend.

Problems of the Sierra are as deceptively benign as the stocking of fish, a more complicated matter than I ever realized when I used to go casting for whatever I could catch—especially happy to fry up a pan full of trout. Only twenty of the Sierra's four thousand high-elevation lakes naturally supported fish. In their absence, a diverse range of invertebrates and amphibians such as the mountain yellow-legged frog had thrived for eons. But during the past century, two thousand high-country lakes were stocked with trout. Exotic to the region, the sleek, popular game fish were even dropped into many lakes from planes flying overhead, upsetting the ancient balance of life with all the discrimination of crop dusters. As a result, the frogs are now gone from many lakes and are biologically endangered throughout their range. They're holding their own in some lakes where stocking has been discontinued or where the artificially planted trout have been eliminated.

Salmon, once plentiful in the rivers of the Sierra and a keystone of whole ecosystems, have come even closer to extinction. Dams eliminated 90 percent of the historic spawning areas. Two unnecessary dams, built solely for the purpose of trapping silt from the mining era, still block the lingering but threatened runs in the Yuba basin. Few people even remember the San Joaquin's once-robust fishery, but conservation groups now work to restore salmon there and in the Yuba.

Owing to pollution, dams, diversions, and damage to whole watersheds, half the Sierra's total native fish and amphibian populations are now at risk of eventual extinction. Waterfront habitats—the most important of all for wildlife—are the most altered and impaired of all lands. Fortunately, the waterfronts can be protected and restored through floodplain zoning to halt development, through setbacks to prevent logging at streamsides, and through the acquisition of key parcels as open space. But none of these solutions are happening fast enough.

Much of the water in Sierra rivers flows from forests that cover the mountains' mid-elevations, but more than 75 percent of those forests have been logged without adequate concern for the health of the watersheds, the soil, the wildlife, and the succeeding forests to come. Very little old-growth forest can be found outside national parks and wilderness areas. Steep slopes have eroded into the streams after timber companies cut the trees. Ancient forests have been reduced to fragments—where they haven't been mowed down like lawns. Large uncut tracts, however, are essential to the endangered wolverine, the rare fisher, the secretive pine marten, the threatened spotted owl, and other forms of life. Five vertebrate species that depend on old-growth forests are at risk of extinction. Closer to home, widespread clear-cutting has dramatically increased the risk of fires, and damage to houses and property has escalated as blazes have become catastrophic. According to the *Sierra Nevada Ecosystem Project Report*, timber harvest has increased fire severity more than any other recent human activity.

As a consequence of my Stanislaus experience, I set out to learn everything that I could about all these problems of the Sierra, and in 1988 I wrote a book called *The Sierra Nevada: A Mountain Journey*. I traveled the length of the range and reported on everything that I saw. Back then, I realized that we needed to view the Sierra as one place so that land managers and all Californians could understand the importance and vulnerability of the mountains. We all needed to better understand the connections, the problems, and the possibilities. In the years between that book and this one, the connections have grown more apparent, the problems more extreme, the possibilities more important.

Reporting on a host of threats in 1991, *Sacramento Bee* journalist Tom Knudson wrote a Pulitzer Prize–winning series called "The Sierra in Peril." His hard-hitting coverage struck a lot of sensitive nerves, and state agencies as well as citizen organizations plotted reform strategies and persuaded Congress to authorize the *Sierra Nevada Ecosystems Project Report*. For the first time, a scientific review of the Sierra was assembled and published—a two-thousand-page document released in 1996.

After years of study, public review, and hearings, the Forest Service, in 2001, responded to the ecosystem analysis with its own landmark document, the National Forest "Framework Plan." This limited the logging of old-growth trees and reformed resource management in profound ways.

Widely considered the most ecologically accountable and scientifically based plan ever done by the Forest Service, the Framework was supported by hundreds of scientists—by nearly all the scientists who took the time to read the plan. But the Bush administration promptly rescinded key provisions, deleting protections for wildlife and watersheds. In 2005 the administration sought to double or triple the amount of logging, spinning to the public a "forest health" rationale purportedly based on thinning for fires but in fact doing the worst possible thing by allowing the cutting of large trees up to thirty inches in diameter. The urgent need to thin the tangle of fire-prone vegetation near communities was bypassed; coping with this problem offered little advantage to timber corporations. Instead, politics trumped science and large pine and fir trees were slated to be commercially logged, even in the 328,000-acre Giant Sequoia National Monument, designated for protection by President Clinton in 2000.

And surpassing even the importance of the forests' fate—in fact determining that fate in ominous ways—air pollution unimagined just a couple of decades ago now plagues the Sierra.

Just like storms, the smog of urban and agricultural California drifts up the western slope with the prevailing winds. Acting on hydrocarbons and nitrogen oxides generated by the burning of fossil fuels—most commonly in cars, trucks, and sport-utility vehicles—the sun alters the chemical makeup of the pollution and produces ozone, which in the lower atmosphere is toxic to plants and hazardous to human health. Ponderosa and Jeffrey pines show widespread damage; giant sequoia seedlings suffer as well. The sun-baked ozone reaches its apex at the 2,000-to-4,000-foot elevation, where it is even worse than in the cities. The American Lung Association's air-pollution report cards flatly failed most west-side Sierra counties, and in 2006 found Bakersfield to be the worst smog source in the nation. Five of the ten worst sources in America were in California—all of them upwind from the Sierra. Harboring the largest organisms on earth, and some of the oldest, Sequoia National Park has the dubious distinction of being the most polluted major national park. From lookouts in the mountains—especially in the south—the layer of deadly smog can be seen every day like a bank of yellow-gray fog building in the valley and wafting up through the foothills to poison the forests and enhaze the great peaks.

Thoroughly enmeshed with this problem, global warming also threatens the Sierra with extreme consequences. Our burning of oil and other fossil fuels has boosted atmospheric carbon, causing an artificial greenhouse effect; the accumulating carbon layer acts like a blanket and a reflector, trapping heat near the earth's surface. The issue has been studied by thousands of scientists, including those at the Pentagon, and nearly all but those paid by oil and coal companies agree that global warming poses dire threats to our climate, our economy, and our security. Globally, 1995 ranked as the earth's hottest year on record, which alarmed people. But then the record was broken in 1997. Then it was broken in 1998, 2001, 2002, 2003, 2004, and 2005. In 2006, the California heat wave made national news for weeks and baked the state's population under a shroud of smog.

A hundred-nation Intergovernmental Panel on Climate Change convened by the United Nations attributed global warming to human activities and made shocking estimates about how bad the situation will become, especially if corrective actions are not taken. With our high consumption levels, the United States is by far the largest source of the problem. But the Bush administration, heavily backed by energy corporations such as the ones that the president and vice president used to work for and continued to get money from, persisted in denying the importance of the issue. Our government stonewalled the nearly unanimous efforts of one hundred and fifty other nations to reduce

global warming. Working in tandem with the federal administration, the energy cartel flooded the media with deceptive accounts that confused the public about the nature and severity of the problem.

Relatively free of political influence, the Scripps Institute predicted that because of global warming, the Sierra snowpack will be reduced one-third by 2060 and halved by 2090. A team of prestigious scientists reported in the *Proceedings of the National Academy of Sciences* in August 2004 that the Sierra snowpack will likely be reduced by 30 to 90 percent by the end of the century as more precipitation comes as rain rather than snow. Within that time, the elevation at which snow is encountered is likely to rise 1,500 feet. This means that there will be *no snow* over many parts of the Sierra where we now find it.

Through its snowpack and river system, the Sierra Nevada now accounts for 48 percent of all the runoff in California, 70 percent of the water supply used by California farms and cities, and most of the water used in northern Nevada. This water is stored for months at a time in the Sierra snowpack, complemented by a system of reservoirs that are filled when the runoff is high and drained when runoff is low. Without the snowpack extending the runoff season until midsummer, and without major improvements in the efficiency with which we use water, the existing storage will be inadequate. With less snow, and with the snow melting sooner, the need for urban and farm water storage will grow, creating new pressure to dam rivers even though the costs will be extreme. The short-term potential of improving efficiency and stretching supplies another twenty years or so offers little in terms of a long-range solution.

The impending lack of water storage is only one among many expected consequences of global warming; the pulpiest science fiction could hardly conjure up a more ominous set of calamities. Floods disgorging into the Central Valley from the Sierra will be worsened as more precipitation comes in the form of rain instead of snow. The climate will be hotter, the summers drier. The sweltering heat of today in places such as Fresno, Redding, and Bakersfield will become the killing heat of tomorrow. Many plants will be driven to extinction, and along with them, wildlife. Weather will become more

VALLEY OAKS NEAR LOWER MERCED RIVER
Valley oaks grow to four feet in diameter—the largest oak species in the West. This middle-aged tree soaks up morning sun in the Sierra's lower foothills. Oak woodlands support the most diverse cast of wildlife in California but are among the most threatened of all ecosystems, owing to mounting development pressures. Population is expected to quadruple in the western foothills by 2040.

erratic, with extended droughts making those of the past look minor. Thunderstorms, and therefore fires, will be more plentiful, and efforts to control them an expensive formality based more on laws about liability than on realistic appraisals of what firefighters can do. The extent and heat of the fires will intensify as they burn larger tracts of forest, increasing threats to towns and the proliferating maze of rural foothill development. Exotic weeds, from places such as Afghanistan and Spain, are well suited to the drier climate and will oust native plants, pasture, and forests, and they will be even more troublesome in the wake of the fires. The accumulated global warming, floods, droughts, fires, weeds, and extinctions will aggravate wicked feedback loops that all spiral downward.

On top of the predictions for warming, scientists have discovered that naturally occurring droughts in the Sierra persisted for hundreds of years in prehistoric times. The combined effect of human-caused warming, natural cycles of drought, degraded ecosystems, and increasing population is one of truly staggering dimensions.

We've damaged or broken the carbon cycle, the fire cycle, the hydrologic cycle, the nitrogen cycle, the migration cycle—even the storm cycle, because the weather is changing as a result of global warming. Yet each of these cycles is essential to the mountains and to people throughout California. The changes raise nettlesome questions as we try to repair the damage we've wreaked on all the vital systems of life.

Underlying all those changes, an ever-growing population is the fundamental cause of fossil fuel consumption, global warming, air pollution, damming, clear-cutting, and the replacement of wildlife habitat with houses and strip malls.

Population of the Sierra doubled—100 percent growth—between 1970 and 1990. That compares to a 49 percent growth rate statewide, which itself ranks as one of the highest in the world (the U.S. rate was 22 percent—by far the highest among industrialized nations and greater than that of many undeveloped countries).

Most people who become Californians also aspire—at least in part—to the California "standard of living," which means consumption of resources and fossil fuel far beyond the amounts they used in their countries of origin—indeed, far beyond the amounts used anywhere else in the world. For example, we use forty times per capita the resources used in India.

Within the context of runaway statewide growth, the Sierra has become a hotspot of new development not only because of the "pull" of desirable places to live, but also because of the "push"—people in extraordinary numbers are fleeing from the increasingly crowded, hot, troubled urban areas where traffic reaches gridlock, and where the hospitals, schools, and law enforcement agencies are broke. Concentrated on the one-third of the Sierra region that is privately owned, a Sierra-wide population of 650,000 is expected to triple by 2040.

In Martis Valley, just north of Lake Tahoe, Placer County approved six thousand new lots in a single subdivision—bigger than the whole nearby town of Truckee. Court challenges greatly reduced the size of the development, but it will still be built. At the border of the Spenceville Wildlife Management Area in the northern foothills, a proposed 5,100-home subdivision would transform California's most critical wildlife habitat—oak woodlands—into the sprawl seen at the edge of every California city. Ground-zero in the fate of oak woodlands, a 36,000-acre new town is proposed in Tulare County's Yokohl Valley and is facilitated by a proposed county plan revision that would fast-track "new towns" wherever anyone wanted to build them. Perhaps most outrageous to Sierra enthusiasts, twenty-seven luxury homes have been approved on the approach to Mount Whitney—virtually at the gate of America's greatest mountain. Lawsuits and proposals to move the development elsewhere are pending.

Nearly every Sierra town experiences extreme growth pressures. Demographers predict that the foothills zone will quadruple in population by 2040. New homesites springing up in fire-prone woodlands, incendiary chaparral, and hazardous floodplains usurp habitat for wildlife, which is pushed back farther and farther onto fewer and fewer acres that are less and less suitable. As more homes go up in deer habitat—and therefore lion habitat—the incidence of mountain lions attacking people may increase. The lions will be blamed for the problem. Meanwhile, domestic cats and dogs that come with the new rural residents decimate local bird populations and small mammals by the millions, with repercussions felt throughout the ecosystem.

The California Department of Finance forecasts that the state's population will double in about thirty-seven years. This is the equivalent of a new Los Angeles every decade. Statewide, more than 90 percent of population growth owes to immigration from other countries and to children of the new immigrants, according to data from the California Department of Finance and the U.S. Census Bureau. Between 1990 and 2000 California's rate of growth was 26 percent. If such growth continues, the population of the state in 2090 will be a staggering 302 million—more than the entire U.S. in 2006. As unrealistic as that projection may seem, little is being done to change the rate of growth.

To cope with the problems of development, the Sierra Nevada Alliance and other groups supporting growth management wisely advocate a four-point program: the maintenance of compact town centers to minimize sprawl, preservation of critical open space, restoration of natural areas, and sustainable "working" use of ranch lands and forests without development.

The people coping with these problems say that to turn the tide against rampant development, the Sierra needs state-of-the-art planning, generous investments in open space, and decisive political will to change business-as-usual. Yet most of the county land-use plans are outdated and inadequate to address the current threats; 85 percent lack provisions to conserve habitat, according to the Alliance's *Planning for the Future*. Spending for protection of the Sierra was less than 1 percent of the state's conservation budget between 1996 and 2001.

And, far from expressing the political will to change, Sierra legislators are among California's most politically conservative.

The challenges of good land management are formidable, but even if the most demanding requirements of planning, funding, and politics were miraculously met, the simple rate of growth in California would still be overwhelming. Even if everyone achieved state-of-the-art efficiency in resource use, the current growth rate would outstrip whatever progressive advances might be made. For example, if per capita use of water were halved, that hard-earned gain would be canceled out by the expected tripling of the Sierra population by 2040 and the doubling of population statewide.

People who recognize the nature of this phenomenon ask, "If the problems are difficult to cope with now—and they are—then what will they be like when the pressures for development double, triple, and quadruple?" The troubling answer is difficult to avoid: whatever is saved today may simply be used up tomorrow, when the demands for everything are acutely greater.

As long as the population of California continues to grow, the pressures for development in the Sierra will also grow. The demands on water and forests will increase. The amount of air pollution will worsen, and the problems of global warming will intensify. Yet few people are even willing to discuss the overriding demographic forces that affect virtually everything.

Though they rarely address population growth as the underlying cause of the Sierra's difficulties, dozens of organizations and thousands of people strive to protect what's left of the mountains and to restore what has been lost.

The Sierra Nevada Alliance represents eighty organizations and finds common ground among divergent groups in its efforts to reform the way we treat the land. Dozens of watershed associations work for the good of their streams. Friends of the River lobbies for river protection. The South Yuba River Citizens League organizes for salmon restoration. The Tuolumne River Trust fights to prevent additional water withdrawals where they would devastate that great river's ecosystem.

Local chapters of the Sierra Club address a broad range of issues. The League to Save Lake Tahoe labors to reverse the tide of loss in the deep blue lake. Eighty organizations have also joined as the Sierra Nevada Forest Protection Campaign to improve forest management.

The California Wilderness Coalition and hundreds of affiliated groups launched the California Wild Heritage Campaign, aiming to designate 2.4 million acres as wilderness on federal land statewide (7 million qualify as wilderness but remain unprotected).

There *is* hope. People who want to protect the mountains could hardly do anything easier and more effective than simply voting for a politician such as California Attorney General Bill Lockyer. Taking courageous stands, he challenged the U.S. Forest Service over its retrograde policy of abandoning the Framework Plan. He filed charges against an irrigation district for grossly polluting Sierra streams in 2002. He worked to protect Lake Tahoe and the embattled Giant Sequoia National Monument.

The combined work of all these organizations and people constitutes the greatest movement ever to protect the Sierra, and responding to that, the legislature and governor in 2004 established the Sierra Nevada Conservancy—a state agency with a mandate for better stewardship.

In spite of onerous problems, conservationists have labored in the Sierra ever since John Muir's first campaign to establish Yosemite National Park. They've succeeded in designating 3.5 million acres of federal land in the Sierra as wilderness and safeguarding fourteen rivers and tributaries in the National Wild and Scenic Rivers system. People here have saved many of the finest samples of nature in America. The Sierra has inspired all this work, and it will no doubt continue to inspire people to cope with even greater challenges in the years ahead.

Unfortunately, rapid population growth makes it harder and harder to succeed. If the booming growth of population in California can be slowed, then there would be real hope for a Sierra Nevada where nature thrives and where the beauty and health of the mountains remain for everyone to use, to enjoy, and to pass on to the next generation.

The river rushed past, as beautiful as flowing water can be. I had just reached the bottom of the Grand Canyon of the Tuolumne, at the end of my first day on a walk through Yosemite.

When people think of this great national park, they usually picture the glaciated cliffs of Yosemite Valley, and so do I. But this time I wanted to get a more complete perspective—to see the valley within the context of all the terrain around it—and so I had embarked on a weeklong trip.

The spectacular upper watersheds of the Tuolumne and Merced Rivers define the park's boundary to the north and east. I planned to hike up the Tuolumne, over the high pass separating the two basins, and down the Merced to the famed valley.

The trail crossed the Tuolumne only two miles above Hetch Hetchy Reservoir, though from the path I saw no sign of America's inaugural conflict over the preservation of parkland, rivers, and wilderness. Formed by a dam built in 1923, the reservoir now floods the closest thing we ever had to another Yosemite Valley. John Muir fought to save this place in the final battle of his life, but lost, and the city of San Francisco built the dam in the nation's third national park and

buried one of the greatest masterpieces of American landscape. The reservoir came to signify everything that a national park should not be—a completely altered landscape for the sake of commodity use and consumption.

Conservationists later reversed this precedent, and the national parks have been protected from additional large dams. Today, with renewed interest in John Muir's final cause, an organization called Restore Hetch Hetchy is making the case for replacing San Francisco's water by other means, dismantling the dam, and restoring the valley. San Francisco, of course, does not want to give up what it has.

In the canyon above Hetch Hetchy, the river still runs free, and as I watched, the crystal-clear flow slicked into pour-overs, bubbled through slots and chutes, tensed in a crescendo of rumbling foam, and exploded with both watery percussion and full-fledged flight at waterfalls—each one more spectacular than the last. The ponderosa pines grew large and the needles and cones smelled like cinnamon rolls when I stopped and sat happily on the ground.

Two days of hiking upstream took me to Tuolumne Meadows, reached by most people via the Tioga Pass road—the highest highway pass in the Sierra and the last one for one hundred and forty miles for people driving southward. Here lies the range's largest meadow, an exquisite place of flowered flats, winding river, and granite peaks. I veered southward and continued ascending along the Lyell Fork of the Tuolumne.

Bears posed the chief hazard here, and, sure enough, one came sniffing at my tent in the night, forcing me to get up, yell, shake my ski poles as if I were angry, and throw stones in order to chase him away.

TUOLUMNE RIVER AT CALIFORNIA FALLS
The Tuolumne River jets down the spectacular granite slab that creates California Falls, where cool spray forms a rainbow in morning light.

I had hung my food from an overhead bar that the Park Service built to resist the bears, and my supplies went untouched. (Bear-proof food canisters are now the preferred and required method for protecting food.)

Gaining elevation, my trail skirted Ireland Lake, where I detoured to camp for a night of halcyon solitude, rocky mountains touching the eastern sky.

The next day took me over the spacious open slopes of Tuolumne Pass, and at that high point of my walk, I could appreciate more clearly what had been accomplished by making a national park of the upper reaches of the Merced and Tuolumne Rivers. The health of a river is dependent on what happens to its entire watershed—all the land that drains into the stream—and the decision to protect the upper basins of these two rivers is one of the better choices we've made in the checkered environmental history of California.

The upper watersheds do not, however, constitute the whole ecosystem—a larger area that embraces land needed by the wildlife of the park. Yosemite's deer, for example, migrate down the canyons to the

102

MERCED RIVER BELOW VERNAL FALL
With robust runoff in early summer, the Merced River roars through its conifer-clad canyon above Yosemite Valley.

foothills, and the bighorn sheep on Mount Gibbs winter on lower slopes of the east side.

Recognizing the importance of land surrounding the park, conservationists succeeded in protecting adjacent national forest as the Emigrant Wilderness to the north, Hoover Wilderness to the northeast, and Ansel Adams Wilderness to the southeast. These additions include some of the most spectacular high country in the Sierra, but unfortunately the wildlife-rich lowlands west of the park went unguarded.

Just beyond the park's western boundary, river conservationists fought dam proposals on the Tuolumne below Hetch Hetchy and on the Merced near El Portal in the 1980s. In winning those fights, they persuaded Congress to include both streams in the National Wild and Scenic Rivers system. This helps to safeguard the greater Yosemite ecosystem from dams, but other threats, such as suburbanization at gateway communities, logging in the mid-elevation timber belt, and foul air from all of agricultural and urban California, loom large.

The trail next led me down Fletcher Creek, a Merced River tributary with flumes of powerfully descending water, and then along the Merced itself, which foams over the most remarkable set of waterfalls in America. I leaned over the railing at the top of Nevada Fall and stared straight down 594 feet at the Merced's greatest free-fall. At the base, the water splayed onto granite bedrock and scarcely hesitated on its journey down the west slope of the Sierra.

The number of people on the trail had been building, and at Vernal Fall nearly a hundred stood watching a bubble-filled Merced arc through space and then drop off, seemingly in slow motion because the distance to the bottom was so great. Mist jetted out from places where the water splattered rocks, and it formed a luminous rainbow in the morning sunlight.

On the final day of my walk, I entered Yosemite Valley and braced myself for another sampling of the Sierra's great paradox. My pursuit of scenery went from a solitary quest with breathtaking views at every turn to a social festival and a search for nature behind buildings and parking lots. At Happy Isles, shuttle buses make their busy rounds. I continued walking, wanting the close-up view that traveling by foot affords.

Horse corrals stabled scores of mounts, and the trails were heavily traveled. Tent cities rose from the riverbanks as campgrounds, and the Curry complex of lodges and cabins packed the woods up above. The Ahwahnee Hotel, crafted in stone and timber, stood in luxury, complete with luxury prices, followed by a commercial district packed with shops, the ranger headquarters and warehouses, employee housing, and then another rambling mall of lodges, restaurants, and parking lots at Yosemite Village. All told, the half-mile-wide valley accommodates thirty thousand people on busy days and holds nearly one thousand buildings and thirty miles of roads.

The urbanized Yosemite continues for two miles, with similarities to urban areas elsewhere. This one just happens to be in a valley that many people regard as the most beautiful place in the world.

The key challenge that park planners have faced is to carry out the advice of America's greatest landscape architect, Frederick Law Olmsted, who was commissioned to prepare a plan for the valley soon after Congress set it aside as a state reserve. Olmsted wrote, "The first point to be kept in mind is to preserve and maintain the natural scenery as exactly as possible." The urban amenities were built to accommodate the wishes of urban visitors. Yet in doing this, the Park Service allowed the valley to be changed in ways that Olmsted would not have approved.

After decades of developing a detailed plan and then decades of only nominally implementing it, the National Park Service has recently increased its efforts to relocate some of the development out of the valley and to relieve some of the congestion by providing more shuttle buses to serve visitors who arrive without their cars or refrain from using them in the park. An inexpedient irony here: increased use of buses enables yet more people to come into the park without the deterrent of congestion on the roads, and the numbers of people continue to go up and up. Likewise, limited accommodations within the valley no longer dissuade people from visiting, because all of the towns

around the park have promoted themselves as "gateway" communities. In glossy brochures and on the Internet, they've broadcast the message that Yosemite is their very own, and they've developed dozens of miles of highway frontage with motels and related facilities. Tour buses carry in large numbers of people from all over the world who would never have heard of the park a decade or two ago. As the number of people using Yosemite increases—even without their cars—the challenges facing park rangers will only grow.

While I walked on paved trails, traffic hummed constantly on a highway that eventually connects to every freeway in California. It ran one-way up the south side of the Merced and one-way down the north side, making Yosemite Valley the world's most beautiful median strip.

The valley escaped the flooded fate that buried the wonders of Hetch Hetchy to the north, but it failed to escape other transformations. With a theme common throughout the Sierra but writ large here, the valley represents the finest of nature but not without the complications that great numbers of people bring.

Even so, the magic of the place persists, and millions of people each year have the opportunity to appreciate it. With others, I took the paved trail to Yosemite Falls, and even though it's the most crowded natural feature in the park, it never fails to captivate me: with its three-pitch drop of 2,425 feet, it is considered by many to be the third-highest waterfall in the world.

Beyond the nearby streets of Yosemite Village and its nexus of buildings, cars, and idling buses, I came to the Merced River, glossy and riffling with granite domes and sheer walls all around. Just beyond lay Leidig Meadow, which I entered not from the road but from a winding, pine-needle path along the river.

Immediately I felt that I had entered a world apart from the bustle and the traffic—a world more like all of Yosemite Valley once was.

A dozen people slowly strolled alone, or in pairs, or in small family groups. The meadow stretched farther than I would have guessed; couples at the other end looked like miniatures. Nobody talked loudly or violated the sublime hush over the place. Blissfully free of sound,

YOSEMITE VALLEY FROM HALF DOME
Many people consider Yosemite Valley the most beautiful place in the world. Here it is seen from the top of Half Dome, 5,000 feet above the valley floor.

the landscape seemed frozen in time, except for the inescapable white noise of the highway, fortunately hidden behind a buffer of forest.

A tall ponderosa pine stood near the northern edge of the meadow. I walked around the tree and admired its station in the world. I reflected on its lifetime spent in that one astonishing place. John Muir would have known this tree exactly as I do. The 4,800-foot face of Half Dome and its sheer granite wall dominated upstream, four miles away, though the size of the monolith made the distance look half as far. Across the valley, Sentinel Rock caught the elegant light of the evening. Downstream, Cathedral Rocks—well named—rose high. Domes and distant summits rimmed the valley and completed the Shangri-la effect.

I leaned against the great tree, smelling its sap and its life, and I thought about nothing but the world immediately around me, and how the remarkable valley had been carved so masterfully by ice, and how the Merced now curves so perfectly with glassy waters, and how, to me, this quiet and unforgettable place is the heart of Yosemite.

YOSEMITE FALL AND BACKWATER OF THE MERCED RIVER
A white alder tree is reflected in placid backwaters of the Merced when the river overtops it banks.

Setting out on the expedition of my dreams, I wanted to see as much of the Sierra as I could, to travel slowly, and to notice the light and the life of every single day. With my wife, Ann, I would walk southward along the crest and through the high country for five weeks, a journey that I variously called "The Great Escape," "The Pilgrimage," and finally, "The Ultimate Mountain Experience."

I looked forward to the continuity that our long route offered. I had learned to think of the Sierra not as an eclectic group of destinations, but rather as one connected piece, and now I would get to see it that way as well. Much of the same country can be visited by taking day-hikes from dozens of trailheads along roads, yet I looked forward to a qualitative difference in exploring the mountains nonstop. My sense of belonging here would have a chance to build and accumulate rather than having to be reset at a new starting point every time I stepped out of the car and went through a troubled phase of trying to forget about the world news.

When the idea of an extended trip first came up, Ann jumped at the opportunity. She had been working as a river guide and Outward Bound wilderness instructor when we met, fifteen years before. Her current career as a writer and historian, plus many commitments to the community where we now live, had taken her away from epic adventures more than she liked. Though we knew that it wouldn't all be easy, we were both thrilled with the prospect of traveling through the Sierra Nevada together and sharing every aspect of the experience ahead of us.

As our friend Janet Cohen drove us up to the Pacific Crest Trailhead at Donner Pass, I remembered my first trip to the Sierra, when I said, "Let me out here." A short but memorable walk had followed. Now I was asking to be let out again, only this time I wouldn't be returning to civilization anytime soon.

The term "Sierra crest" suggests a continuous ridge of high country, but this oversimplifies the lay of the land. True, as I have written, the range is unbroken by the low gaps common to America's other great mountain chains: the Appalachians, Rockies, Cascades, Coast Ranges, Alaska, and Brooks. But to travel anywhere in the Sierra requires extensive climbing and descending. Most of the actual crest is far too rugged for walking; if the trail truly stayed there, it would present a hopelessly rugged cliff-hanger course, and so the path repeatedly descends and wanders for miles just to find passable byways around extreme topography. Our route would alternately swap the expansive high view for the closer examination of sheltered forest wilderness, and I looked forward to seeing the whole picture.

Our first climb, toward Mount Judah, had all the tingling anticipation of a new beginning. My boots gripped the stones and dirt underfoot. All my gear plus a week's food supply hung heavily on my shoulders while my pack's belt-strap intercepted some of the weight at my waist. I also carried substantial camera gear in a belt pack attached at my

VOLUNTEER PEAK
In the wilds of northern Yosemite National Park, Volunteer Peak rises west of Benson Pass—a high, rugged divide on the Pacific Crest Trail.

stomach, and a tripod cinched onto my pack. To make hiking a full-body sport, and to guard against slipping, I carried ski poles. The combined load pulled me mercilessly into the earth, my muscles and bones trying to convert the pack's downward push into forward motion. There's nothing like sixty pounds of gear to make me appreciate the ability of my fellow mammals to live out there with nothing but their teeth and fur.

From our first high perch I could see many mountain ridges, sequentially layered out to the horizon, one on top of another until the last one faded like a mirage in the atmosphere. At once enthralled and intimidated, I knew that I would walk the whole way to that far horizon in a few demanding days, and that when I got there, I would see another horizon, just as distant, just as alluring, and that this would happen over and over again, perhaps ten times in all.

As a hiker, I had come to follow this path of the mountains.

As an adventurer, I had come to explore the unknown and to live in the mountain world with all its challenges of terrain and climate.

As a photographer, I had come for both the light and the scenery; without good light, a perfect view does not make a good photo. Because I avoid the now-common option of doctoring my pictures digitally on a computer, and prefer instead to show what I actually see, the only way to get good content along with good light is to be outside a lot. After all is said and done, the best three rules of outdoor photography are "Be there, be there, and be there."

Finally, as a writer, I had come seeking a sense of meaning in these mountains. Without slighting the purely physical or the important nuances in geography, weather, and wildlife, I also hoped to read the Sierra's underlying script. I wanted to discover all that the place might reveal. What do these mountains mean to me? Why are they so important?

Actually launching the trip was a huge relief; the logistical problems for our four-hundred-mile trek, including day-hikes, had been formidable. Ann and I had packed food into boxes for each of the hike's five legs. We mailed three to ourselves, general delivery, at post offices directly on the route, and we sent one to a friend who would drive up

to Sonora Pass and meet us. After emerging from the southern Sierra, we would catch a bus back north to Reno and then return to our van at Janet's house.

We started at Donner Pass, though the Sierra begins seventy-five airline miles farther north, where the first big outcrops of granite now lie flooded beneath Almanor Reservoir. From there to Interstate 80 at Donner, the Sierra shows more brown volcanic rock than granite, more forest than high country. We would miss all of that but, as with the rest of life, we couldn't do it all.

During the first leg of our tour, we walked through forests and meadows west of Lake Tahoe and also along high ridgelines that offered views to the twenty-two-mile-long oval of lake. Even though it was late June, deep snow remained in places and made route-finding difficult; the trail was buried beneath drifts and mounds of snow that clung to north-facing slopes in the shade of conifers. Accumulations still measured six feet and more—steep-sided obstacles that required us to climb up, trudge across, and slide down. Fortunately the snow had settled so densely by freeze-and-thaw action that we never sunk below the tops of our boots.

Entering the Desolation Wilderness, we encountered our first expansive outcrops of granite. Lakes dotted the landscape, and we camped in sight of the elegant landmark Pyramid Peak, familiar from my earlier climb.

The trail south of Highway 50 lured us to meadows at the head-waters of the Truckee River, replete with wildflowers and mosquitoes. South of Carson Pass we skirted the impressive mountain modestly called Round Top, traversed a steep snowfield persisting on the flank of the adjacent "Elephant's Back," and admired deep canyons yawning toward the Mokelumne River.

Roaming pack-free in the evening, when low sunlight cast a luminous glow so characteristic of the Sierra, I knew that mountains certainly mean beauty, and with my camera I sought to capture it as best I could.

I knew that natural beauty makes me feel good. Furthermore, I regard it as essential to a positive view on life; I cannot imagine having a good attitude if I were surrounded only by ugliness. I've long suspected that some of the problems of our society stem from a chronic lack of beauty and a rising flood of ugliness all around us. But now I wondered, just what makes the mountains seem so beautiful? Of course, beauty just *is*, and the colors, shapes, textures, light, and elegant composition found everywhere in the Sierra are all integral. But beyond that, I thought about evolutionary imperatives and the surprising linkage they may have to aesthetic sensibilities.

Geographer Jay Appleton has outlined a fascinating theory that people evolved with an affinity for the kinds of places that enabled them to survive. He reasoned that a marriage of prospect and refuge is critical in the landscapes we prefer. We need prospect so that we can see out and be aware of approaching danger—wild animals, hostile warriors, stormy weather. At the same time, we need refuge—a place of shelter, comfort, security. Landscapes that offer both prospect and refuge appeal to us powerfully for reasons rooted deeply in our past.

Neither Appleton nor I is an evolutionary biologist, but when I looked around to informally appraise his theory, I thought it rang true. Often the scenes that struck me as the most beautiful offered a sense of refuge within a frame of old pine trees or wind-sheltering granite. They also looked out to distant panoramas where I could view the larger world.

I also thought about biologist Edward O. Wilson's similar theory of biophilia. Wilson suggests that we are drawn to nature—and to love it—because it works ecologically and therefore has the ability to support us and our needs for food, water, and shelter. In other words, we love nature because it enables us to live. As my own corollary to this idea, I reasoned that the natural world looks beautiful because it works for us. Landscapes that still function with nature's essential cycles intact look better than places where the cycles are broken. In short, healthy landscapes look better than ruined ones. My own experience in the Sierra constantly showed me an abundance of life in flowers and trees, a refreshment of flowing streams, and a landscape that nourished everything around it. Each natural scene looked simply splendid to me and, sure enough, each revealed whole systems of life that still worked well: soil nourishing plants, plants feeding animals, birds eating bugs, sunlight and water suffused throughout as the ultimate life forces.

The mountains surely signified beauty to me, but it would be a whitewash to say they didn't also signal hardship. Sierra history is rife with stories of pain and deprivation up there. Our trip, too, had its difficulties, though they were relatively minor. Not only did remaining snow obscure the trail in places, but at high passes we had to climb or traverse steep snowbound slopes where a slip of the foot could mean an uncontrolled downward slide of a thousand feet—rocks at the bottom. Prepared for such hazards, we each unstrapped a lightweight ice ax, tied it tightly to the end of a ski pole, and only then proceeded to kick tenuous steps into the hardened crust. If either of us were to fall, we would dig the pick-like end of the ice ax into the snow to stop our downward slide. Or so we hoped.

No sooner had the snowpack receded than mosquitoes emerged by the millions, perhaps billions, requiring us to keep covered with clothes, including gloves. We smeared citronella oil on exposed skin and we occasionally resorted to stronger repellents and hid our faces in head-nets. We even put up our bug-net tent for lunch on some days.

Every day, the gradient of the Sierra forced us to sweat, tested our endurance, and occasionally caused us to feel that we were wearing down rather than gaining in strength as the weeks passed. But in overcoming these hardships, I somehow felt more alive, more vital. The pleasures that remained seemed all the sweeter by way of contrast, and we were constantly rewarded for our efforts with scenes that changed by the mile.

South of Carson Pass and the bouldered maze of Border Ruffian Flat, we walked beneath volcanic summits adorned with the pinnacles and spires of a fantasy world. Sheltered forests of red firs yielded to magnificently lighted groves of scattered western white pines, then to sunny gardens of rockbound junipers—charismatic beyond any other species, owing to centuries of slow growth sculpted by the harsh elements of Sierra climate.

Beyond Ebbetts Pass we continued to gain elevation, and as we approached Sonora Pass the country opened across treeless plateaus and breezy knobs. Wind-flattened thickets of whitebark pines had been planted, no doubt, by Clark's nutcrackers. On one high ridgeline, powerful updrafts made us feel that we could almost take flight. The wind increased as we climbed, giving us the exhilarating chill that accompanies high summits along with the suspense of not knowing what lay ahead in the vigorous system of mountain weather.

The mountains continued to grow higher as we advanced southward, and as the views expanded, it became clear to me that—beyond the polarities of beauty and hardship—mountains mean an opportunity for exploration and adventure that is rare in today's world. As we traversed that high country with its full sweep of wildness, I felt thrilled to have so much that was unknown still ahead of me. I'm not sure why the unknown stirred me so—perhaps because it presented the opportunity to learn—to gain understanding by simply seeing what the earth had to offer. Each view was unlike any other I had ever seen, and simply walking through new terrain felt like an accomplishment. Each day, I thought I understood my world a little better, if only by better knowing the beauty that is there.

An old friend, Steve Brougher, generously drove our next food box up from his home near Sonora, the surrounding country familiar to him from his days as a backcountry ranger and biologist for the Forest Service. Steve has since taken up the challenge of ridding his beloved Emigrant Wilderness—a virtual extension of northern Yosemite National Park—of eighteen useless but costly low

TUOLUMNE FALLS
The Tuolumne mists the morning sunrise above Glen Aulin.

110

dams cobbled together a century ago at the outlets of high-country lakes. He encounters opposition from people who like the dams, and who think that dams belong in the wilderness, and who believe that stocked trout need the structures even though fisheries studies show that they do not.

Reluctantly saying good-bye to Steve, we climbed steeply from Sonora Pass, and from the ridge to its south I could see dozens of peaks serrating the far edge of sky. Beyond the Emigrant Wilderness lay the remote backcountry of Yosemite. To the west, the Central Valley and urban California lay too distant to be seen, though the low-lying smog—thickening as we moved southward—offered evidence of what was there.

I knew that the mountains meant a chance to explore and to search for adventure and beauty in everything around me, and now, mostly isolated from the rest of the world, the Sierra also struck me as nature's refuge from whatever was happening down below. Whole systems of life have been eradicated at lower elevations but survive up here. Likewise,

BANNER PEAK IN THE ANSEL ADAMS WILDERNESS
An evening thunderstorm dissipates behind Banner Peak and the rock-studded intricacy of Thousand Island Lake.

the mountains were a refuge for me and for other people wanting to escape the maw of sprawl and motors. In every place I had lived down below—even the most pleasant neighborhoods—I had found that the white noise of the freeways was virtually inescapable. I call it the "roar of California." Now, from my windy perch, that situation struck me as a strange marriage of normalcy and madness. The loss of nature, and everything it entails, is largely regarded as normal down below, and surely this is as mad as any of our individual psyches gone awry.

Again and again during the coming weeks, I felt the satisfying sense of protection that the mountains offered. While the comfort didn't quell the distress I felt for the problems that literally wafted up to our elevation in a haze far thicker than it used to be, I was satisfied to know that a place of even partial refuge still exists, both for the life of the mountains and for the refreshment and hope it offers to me and others.

We can go to the Sierra to see that nature survives. Here the enduring cycles of weather and water, seismic uplift and attrition by rockfall, births of billions of organisms followed by their inevitable death, decay, and recycling reminded me that the mountains benefit all life.

I could now see far southward to the twin summits of Banner Peak and Mount Ritter—rocky toothed landmarks of the central Sierra. The whole skyline enticed us onward as the mountains ramped upward; the passes between the peaks now lay higher than the summits had been during the first week of our trip.

Increasingly wild in a new level of rugged severity, the Yosemite backcountry challenged us with its coarse grain of southwest-dropping canyons angled at ninety degrees to our line of travel. The rigorous trail led us up and down, up and down. Catching our breath, we paused for longer interludes to rest, to look, and to wonder. Granite gleamed all

around us, and canyons with names such as Matterhorn resembled small versions of Yosemite itself.

Emerging from this great wilderness at the end of a grueling, mosquito-infested day, we approached the Tuolumne River and began to feel refreshed by the bubbling sound alone. We made our camp in a remote spot, walked down to the river, took off our sweaty clothes, and carefully slipped into a protected eddy for a moonlight dip on the warm summer night. The cold rushing water renewed us, and as the night closed in, we decided that this magnificent wild river was a perfect climax to the first half of our trip.

Between the popular destination of Tuolumne Meadows, where the Tioga Pass highway was the last road to cross our route, and the recreational magnet of Mammoth Mountain, which is the most-used ski area in America, we saw many other hikers. We stood awestruck above the shores of Thousand Island Lake as the latest in a series of evening thunderstorms cleared and a rainbow arched across the flanks of Banner Peak—no longer a distant tooth on the horizon but rather a towering monolith that rose point-blank in front of us.

Beyond Mammoth we walked through brilliant high basins, down precipitous canyon slopes, across streams bursting with pure snowmelt, and past riots of wildflowers peaking in bloom. All this lay in the John Muir Wilderness.

The massive size of the surrounding wild country enthralled me, though I knew that it wasn't much compared to what is needed nationwide, or even statewide, or even in the Sierra Nevada. Only 12 percent of the United States is protected as wilderness, national parks, or wildlife refuges. Many entire ecosystems across the country are not protected at all. Yet conservation biologists recommend that half the land should be safeguarded to some degree if the fundamental systems of life are to survive, let alone flourish. The high Sierra is relatively well protected—better than almost any other region in America. A comparable length of wilderness—running one hundred and forty continuous miles along the Sierra crest—is found nowhere else outside Alaska. Yet I knew that our ecosystem also entails lower country, such as the oak woodlands used by deer in winter. Though they are one of the most critical types of habitat, less than 1 percent of the oak woodlands of the Sierra are protected. Offering hope, the California Wild Heritage Campaign lobbies for wilderness designation of several hundred thousand acres of federal land in the Sierra.

We camped in the high basin of Evolution Creek, elegant with its smooth sweep of rock, its sheen of lakes, its warmth of evening light. The next morning we climbed to Muir Pass, then descended the steep headwaters of the Middle Fork Kings. Here the wildness intensified in an utter chaos of landscape still being formed—glacial scrapings in piles of unsorted boulders, random rockslides still finding their angles of repose, melting snowbanks that measured twenty feet deep even in August, sudsing waterfalls sweeping away everything that touched them, and darkened ice tunnels where whole streams were sucked under mountainous piles of dirty-white avalanche debris, and then disappeared. All this funneled down to the sublime LeConte Canyon, which—more than any other place—struck me as the wild heart of the Sierra.

In the upper reaches of that great granite watershed—up where the terrain is highest and where the Kings River starts—I felt that the mountains were truly a source. They marked the source not only of water that plunged freely down spectacular slopes, but also of silt and soil that fill the valleys below, of rain and snow that fall because of the Sierra's towering rise into the clouds, and of whole communities of creatures that find refuge here and nowhere else.

I tried to imagine how different the isolation of that great basin would have felt if the city of Los Angeles had been successful with its 1952 hydroelectric proposal to dam the Kings and its forks in five different places. The reservoirs, transmission lines, and roads would have made a gaping hole in the greatest wilderness of the Sierra, transforming it from the source of mountain life that I found to a source of electricity just like any of the others all across America.

Now knowing the unity of the range, I had a better sense of how the loss of any single piece would diminish the whole, and I felt deep gratitude to the people who had made this a national park and saved it as a refuge for nature—rare and unequaled in scale in America.

On the last evening of the hike, as we sat on rocks at the crest of Bishop Pass and watched the sunset light rise from the shining lakes of the Dusy Basin and then climb the western flanks of Aperture Peak, I thought about all we had seen, and how mountain meanings had become clearer to me. I appreciated the beauty that seems integral to a positive outlook on life, the hardship that's needed to fully appreciate pleasure, the escape from the grip of civilization down below, with its troubling partnership of normalcy and madness. Even more, I appreciated a refuge of wildness in which the great systems of life can survive and in which all people can see and experience the natural world.

While other mysteries of existence might remain unsolved for the rest of time, it seemed perfectly clear to me that these mountains were a place of enduring power and a timeless source of life. Surrounded by them, and by the beauty and the challenges that they offered, I felt more alive and more a part of all I had seen and touched. Feeling not separate but forever bonded to the Sierra Nevada and to its primal forces, I knew, beyond all else, that I was happy to be alive.

SUNRISE IN THE EVOLUTION BASIN, KINGS CANYON NATIONAL PARK
Evolution Creek washes over rocky ledges at the base of Mount Haeckel.

RITTER RANGE

Banner Peak and Mount Ritter accent the Ritter Range, seen
here at sunset from Silver Pass, twenty miles to the south.

PINE FOREST ABOVE MIDDLE FORK SAN JOAQUIN
Lodgepole and western white pines endure on rocky slopes
at the headwaters of the Middle Fork San Joaquin River.

MOON OVER THE RITTER RANGE
Just after sunset, a crescent moon drops toward the rugged
western horizon of Iron Mountain and the Ritter Range, seen
here west of Mammoth at Minaret Summit.

DEVILS POSTPILE

One of the finest examples anywhere of columnar basalt, Devils Postpile
formed when lava cooled slowly beneath the surface of the earth. In the
early twentieth century, the unique formation was slated to become
fill for a mining company's dam. Instead, conservationists succeeded in
protecting the site as a National Monument.

Basalt columns

At the top of Devils Postpile, the end-grains of hexagonal basalt columns were exposed by glaciers, which scraped and polished the dark rock.

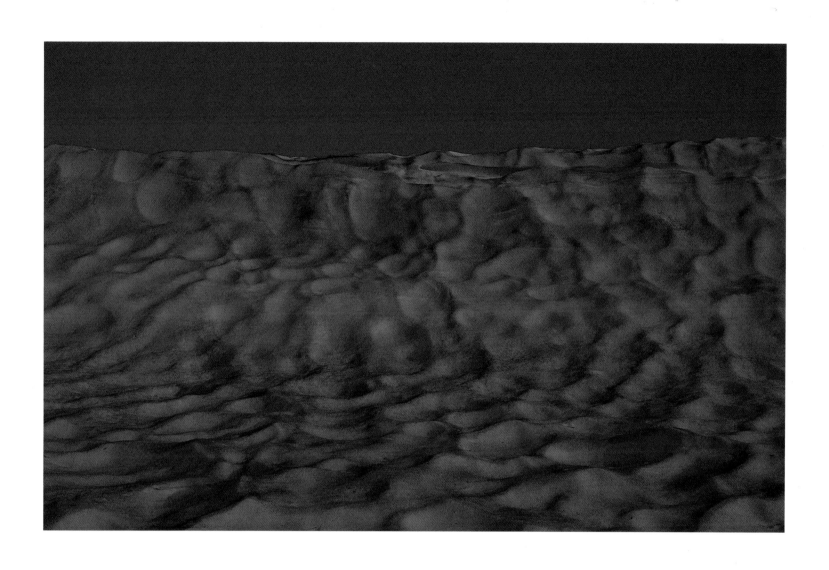

SNOWDRIFT AT SILVER PASS
Settling into ripples as it melts, a deep snowdrift
persists throughout the summer at Silver Pass.

SILVER PASS LAKE IN THE JOHN MUIR WILDERNESS
Silver Pass Lake mirrors walls and pinnacles of granite in the
Sierra high country.

WEST FORK BEAR CREEK

At the outlet of Marie Lake, Bear Creek begins its fabulous descent through steep canyons. Farther downstream, the creek is diverted for hydropower before it reaches the South Fork San Joaquin. Mount Senger looms beneath an afternoon thunderhead.

121

MOUNT HOOPER FROM SELDEN PASS

Rising from the splendor of Selden Pass, and separating Bear Creek from the South Fork San Joaquin drainage, Mount Hooper basks in morning light while clouds from a southern storm gather overhead.

HUMPHREYS BASIN IN WINTER

Humphreys Basin, suffused in the monochrome of winter,
rolls westward from Piute Pass, in the John Muir Wilderness.

Marmot

At home in high country, a yellow-bellied
marmot ventures out of its rocky shelter
to feed on forbs at timberline.

MOUNT MENDEL IN THE EVOLUTION BASIN
Mount Mendel reaches toward the sky above Evolution Basin,
where expansive granite bedrock is rimmed by breathtaking peaks.

Ansel Adams Wilderness

Balloon Dome separates the Middle and South Fork basins of the San Joaquin River, seen from this remote spot near the French Trail, southeast of Bass Lake.

VALLEY OAK AND WESTERN FOOTHILLS
Emblematic of the Sierra's low-elevation foothills, valley oaks crown the western foothills near Eastman Reservoir, north of Fresno. This is one of few oak savannas protected by public ownership.

KINGS RIVER
At the height of springtime, the Kings River winds through a foothill savanna of grassland and valley oaks on the west slope of the Sierra.

CALIFORNIA POPPIES ABOVE THE KINGS RIVER
Poppies and lupines bloom on grassy foothills above the Kings River upstream from its North Fork confluence.

SYCAMORES AND THE KINGS RIVER
Requiring the moisture of floodplain soils, California sycamores reach for sunlight with contorted limbs in this slough of the Kings River upstream from Pine Flat Reservoir.

WILD ONIONS IN KINGS CANYON NATIONAL PARK
Wild onions mix with ferns at the headwaters of the Middle Fork Kings River.

GIANT SEQUOIAS IN SEQUOIA NATIONAL PARK
In the Giant Forest area, this grove of sequoias has prevailed throughout
the ages. Seventy-five groves of the great trees can be found from the
Kern River basin in the south to the Middle Fork of the American.

GIANT SEQUOIAS IN KINGS CANYON NATIONAL PARK
The afternoon sun sends shafts of spare autumn light
through an ancient grove of sequoias in Redwood Canyon.

MOOSE LAKE, SEQUOIA NATIONAL PARK
A full moon rises in the remote backcountry of Sequoia National Park; Mount Stewart and the Great Western Divide rise in the distance.

135

**FOXTAIL PINES NEAR THE
GREAT WESTERN DIVIDE**
Heavy winds shape ancient foxtail
pines west of Elizabeth Pass, at the
headwaters of the Middle Fork
Kaweah River.

MARBLE FORK, KAWEAH RIVER
Crystal clear in autumn, the Marble Fork of the Kaweah pools
momentarily near Lodgepole, in Sequoia National Park.

MORO ROCK, IN SEQUOIA NATIONAL PARK

The setting sun shines on Moro Rock—a monolith of granite facing the Central Valley far below. Castle Rocks rise across the canyon of the Middle Fork Kaweah River, filled with valley fog on this late-autumn afternoon.

EASTERN SIERRA NEAR HOT CREEK

While a winter's accumulation of snow melts on sagebrush flats, clouds arc
into the sky over the Long Valley Caldera, south of Mammoth. Convict Creek
and Mount Morrison lie to the right.

BEAR CREEK SPIRE AND ROCK CREEK CANYON

Reflected in the calm waters of Long Lake, Bear Creek Spire marks the head of the Rock Creek basin in the John Muir Wilderness. Mounts Dade, Abbot, and Mills adjoin to the right.

Snowstorm

The water that comes from the Sierra snowpack is critical to life throughout the mountains, and it provides for much of urban and agricultural California. A winter snowstorm fills the sky and begins to cover lodgepole pines here below Bishop Pass.

TEMPLE CRAG AND NORTH PALISADE

On a sub-zero night in midwinter, the sun drops behind storm clouds
settling on Temple Crag, in the center, and the North Palisade—the Sierra's
third-highest peak—on the horizon at 14,242 feet. This perspective is from
the neighboring White Mountains, north of Westgard Pass.

MOUNT GAYLE

The last sunlight of the day catches the flanks of Temple Crag
while the moon rises over Mount Gayle, west of Big Pine.

OWENS RIVER EAST OF BIG PINE

Kid Mountain, Birch Mountain, and other peaks of the eastern Sierra line the horizon over the Owens River and its rich riparian habitat of Fremont cottonwoods and black willows. Downstream from here the river is dried up by diversions to Los Angeles. The river's historic terminus in Owens Lake has become an alkali dustbed and an air pollution nuisance, but minor reinstatements of flow have allowed some bird species to reinhabit the riverfront and related wetlands.

DOUGLAS-FIR, NORTH FORK OAK CREEK
Douglas-firs thrive in a cool recess along the
Baxter Pass Trail, northwest of Independence.

145

MOUNT WILLIAMSON

In autumn the rusty red of California buckwheat and the yellow gold of rabbitbrush color the arid eastern base of the Sierra. Mount Williamson—second-highest peak in the range at 14,375 feet—ramps up in the background.

TUNNABORA PEAK

The thunder, lightning, and ominous cloud masses of a thunderstorm yield to brilliant bursts of sunlight on Tunnabora Peak, above Wales Lake, just north of Mount Whitney.

DOMELAND WILDERNESS AND THE SOUTH FORK KERN BASIN
The nearly inaccessible canyons of the Domeland Wilderness drain into
tributaries of the South Fork Kern River. Haze and pollution from the
southern Central Valley waft up the canyons in the summertime.

LONE PINE PEAK AND THE ALABAMA HILLS
The first snowstorm of the year has chilled Lone Pine Peak,
reigning over the Alabama Hills west of Lone Pine.

FIVE FINGERS, NORTH OF WALKER PASS

A granite cluster called Five Fingers marks the eastern edge
of the southern Sierra near Walker Pass and Highway 178.

JOSHUA TREES AT INDIAN WELLS CANYON
At its southeastern limits, the Sierra merges with the Mojave
Desert. At this remarkable biological crossroads, high-country
plants mix with desert vegetation, including Joshua trees.

151

ARRASTRE CREEK, SOUTHEAST OF PORTERVILLE
California buckeyes and blue oaks crowd together in the
canyon of Arrastre Creek, a tributary to the White River in the
lower western foothills.

KERN RIVER
The Kern River sieves through intricate boulder gardens,
pushes against undercut rocks, and plunges over waterfalls
along Highway 178. This big drop in the Sierra's southernmost river lies below Democrat Hot Springs.

153

SOUTHERN SIERRA AND THE TEHACHAPI MOUNTAINS
In a final uprising of granite, the outcrops of Piute Peak face the east-west axis of the Tehachapi Range. Here, after four hundred miles of mountain wonders, the Sierra Nevada reaches its end.

SINGLELEAF PINYON ON PIUTE PEAK
Excelling on hot and dry slopes, pinyon pines filter the light of a
rising moon behind Piute Peak—the highest mountain in the
southernmost reaches of the Sierra.

155

To climb Mount Whitney, 14,494 feet above sea level, we awoke at four a.m., gobbled breakfast, and quickly packed in the dark. Then Ann and I strode up the west-side trail by starlight, not a wisp of cloud or moisture in the sky. The white granite all around us reflected the spare light without shading or shadows; the Sierra was subtly luminous even without sunlight.

This final ascent promised to be the climax of an expedition from Cottonwood Creek, south of Whitney, to the isolated splendor of Wales Lake, and then back to Whitney—the highest mountain. This wasn't my first trip to the summit of the Sierra, but it had all the excitement of something I had never done before.

We briefly rested at Hitchcock Lakes and admired the Sierra's yellow glow at daybreak. Then we pressed on, switchbacking upward, our footsteps splintering fragile veneers of ice that had crystallized overnight.

Gaining the Sierra crest and welcoming the warmth of full sunlight, we turned northward on the ridgeline trail and stepped up and up. Pinnacles of granite rose on the right side, and between them we glimpsed a bird's-eye view into the Owens Valley, though the dizzying drop of two miles through space left us clutching for security.

We crossed one more wide slope of broken rock, and we crunched through last winter's final remnant of snowpack, which lingered in a peaked pattern of melting sun cups like meringue on top of a fancy lemon pie.

Deceptively rounded as it pitched down in a convex curve to the west, nearly vertical as it disappeared to the east, America's highest mountain outside Alaska typified the entire Sierra's profile of western incline and eastern escarpment. In this and other ways, Whitney seemed fitting as a crowning symbol of the great range that I had come to see.

Breathing hard in the thinning air, we reached the top. We set our packs on the ground and looked around in wonder at hundreds of other peaks, the entire visible world lower than us. Many summits were identifiable, but many more were not, and they roughened the horizon with the full range of shapes that erosion and the unrelenting strength of gravity can cause—pyramids, flat tops, obelisks, hunchbacks, domes, teeth, claws, bald heads, saw blades, dune-like mounds, whitecaps, breaking waves, and ripples like sand in the bottom of a stream. The peaks were packed together so tightly in the spacious but foreshortened view that the canyons and valleys in between them could hardly be seen, yet we knew that each hosted its own stream or river, its own groves of red firs or lodgepoles, its own mountain hemlocks or charismatic junipers.

We gave each other a big hug and didn't say much, but smiled with a sense of full satisfaction.

We were there.

Because it was still early in the morning, we sat in near solitude on the popular summit, but in this culminating moment of a weeklong

MOUNT WHITNEY FROM THE ALABAMA HILLS
Mount Whitney and neighboring high peaks rise 10,000 vertical feet, nearly two miles, above Lone Pine. Mount Langley lies on the far left, Lone Pine Peak occupies the center, and the more distant vertical spires of Whitney appear on the far right.

trip and a thirty-eight-year-long exploration of the whole Sierra, I hoped that these mountains could be known by many others—not only by people today, but also by those who will come later—even generations from now. Wilderness and nature will surely be just as important then as they are today.

An hour later, clouds with sharply etched tops and dark, soggy bottoms began building above the westward peaks. We had been watching the same pattern for several days, and it invariably led to afternoon thunderstorms at the highest summits. Now I watched the clouds' slow but inevitable approach, and just as I had done years before, on my first walk in the Sierra near Tioga Pass, I asked, "Is there anything to fear?" The beauty of the place was overwhelming, magnetic, seductive. It would have been easy to stay. But now I knew more about the mountains, and so I could not dismiss the danger.

With remarkable sights still awaiting us on safer ground below, we began the long and steep walk down the eastern slope of the Sierra Nevada.

WEST FACE OF MOUNT WHITNEY
Unlike the vertical east face of Whitney, the west side is rounded. Tumbling downward, one of the highest-elevation watercourses on the continent, Whitney Creek, carries snowmelt to the North Fork of the Kern River.

HITCHCOCK LAKES AND SUN CUPS ON MOUNT WHITNEY

Mount Hitchcock and its group of lakes lie southwest of Mount Whitney.
Sun cups—depressions in the snowpack caused by meltwater runoff and
the angle of the snow surface—persist even in August.

MOUNT WHITNEY
Catching the luminous glow of
daybreak, Mount Whitney rises
higher than any other peak in the
United States outside Alaska.

LARKSPURS NEAR BEAR CREEK, SAN JOAQUIN BASIN
Twelve species of larkspurs are native to the Sierra. All have
striking blue flowers. They are poisonous to cattle, but elk
and sheep eat them without harm.

A host of published sources were valuable to me as I wrote *Luminous Mountains*.

My 1988 book, *The Sierra Nevada: A Mountain Journey,* covers many of the places and issues affecting the Sierra in greater depth, and offers an extensive list of publications and interviews that have informed my work.

The single most important source for Sierra information is now the *Sierra Nevada Ecosystem Project Report,* in a summary plus four volumes, published by the Centers for Water and Wildland Resources at the University of California, Davis. Information regarding the following topics was gleaned from the summary, with in-depth coverage found in volumes 1 and 2. For some of the critical topics I have covered—mostly in chapters 4 and 5—see the following pages of the summary:

Population projections, pp. 2, 4
Effect of logging on fires, p. 4
Fire ecology, p. 5
Endangered species and old-growth forests, p. 5
Salmon, p. 8
Riparian habitat, pp. 8, 9
Oak habitat, p. 9
Prehistoric droughts, p. 12

Also of great value, *Sierra Citizen* is a quarterly newspaper published by the South Yuba River Citizens League, in Nevada City. Other useful sources follow.

Beesley, David. *Crow's Range: An Environmental History of the Sierra Nevada.* Carson City: University of Nevada Press, 2005. The first environmental history of the entire Sierra Nevada.

Bouvier, Leon. *California's Population Growth, 1990–2002: Virtually All from Immigration.* Santa Barbara: Californians for Population Stabilization, 2003, p. 4, using California Department of Finance and U.S. Census Bureau data. (Population growth owing to immigration is covered here in chapter 5.)

Browning, Peter. *Place Names of the Sierra Nevada.* Berkeley: Wilderness Press, 1986.

California Nature Conservancy. *Sliding toward Extinction: The State of California's Natural Heritage, 1987.* San Francisco: California Nature Conservancy, 1987. Imperiled species and ecosystems statewide.

Centers for Water and Wildland Resources. *Summary of the Sierra Nevada Ecosystem Project Report.* Davis: University of California, 1996. For further detail, see Volume I, *Assessment Summaries and Management Strategies, Sierra Nevada Ecosystem Project,* and Volume II, *Assessments and Scientific Basis for Management Options.*

Committee to Save the Kings River. *The Kings River: A Report on Its Qualities and Its Future.* Fresno: Committee to Save the Kings River, 1987. Available from Friends of the River.

Duane, Timothy P. *Shaping the Sierra: Nature, Culture, and Conflict in the Changing West.* Berkeley: University of California Press, 1998. Land use changes in the northern Sierra.

Farquhar, Francis P. *History of the Sierra Nevada.* Berkeley: University of California Press, 1965.

Fiddler, Claude, et al. *Yosemite Once Removed: Portraits of the Backcountry.* El Portal: Yosemite Association, 2003. Photos and essays about the Yosemite backcountry.

Hayhoe, Katharine, et al. "Emissions Pathways, Climate Change, and Impacts on California." *Proceedings of the National Academy of Sciences* 101:34 (August 24, 2004). Predictions regarding global warming and the Sierra (covered here in chapter 5).

Hill, Mary. *Geology of the Sierra Nevada.* Berkeley: University of California Press, 1975.

Johnston, Verna R. *Sierra Nevada.* Boston: Houghton Mifflin, 1970. Natural history (covered here in chapter 4).

Keeley, John. "Impact of Fire and Grazing on Diversity and Invasion in Sierran Forests." www.werc.usgs.gov/invasivespecies/sierranfire.html, January 2003 (accessed May 31, 2007). Proliferation of weeds after fires (covered here in chapter 5).

Kellert, Stephen R., and Edward O. Wilson, eds. *The Biophilia Hypothesis.* Washington, D.C.: Island Press, 1993. Includes Professor Wilson's theory of biophilia, mentioned here in chapter 7.

Kennedy, Robert F., Jr. *Crimes against Nature.* New York: HarperCollins, 2004. The Bush administration's response to global warming and other environmental problems.

Knudson, Tom. "The Sierra in Peril." *Sacramento Bee*, special report, June 13, 1991.

Muir, John. *John Muir: The Eight Wilderness-Discovery Books*. Seattle: The Mountaineers, 1992.

———. *The Mountains of California*. New York: Doubleday, 1961. The openness of the forests (pp. 113–114), covered here in chapter 4.

Noss, Reed F., and Allen Y. Cooperrider. *Saving Nature's Legacy*. Washington, D.C.: Island Press, 1994. Half of the land should be protected (p. 168), covered here in chapter 7.

Pacific Rivers Council. *The Urgent Need for Watershed Protection and Restoration in the Sierra Nevada*. Sacramento: Pacific Rivers Council, 1995. Health of fisheries (p. 8), covered here in chapter 5; 70 percent of the water used in California is from the Sierra (p. 6), covered here in chapter 7.

Palmer, Tim, ed. *California's Threatened Environment*. Washington, D.C.: Island Press, 1993. A survey of environmental issues throughout the state.

———. *The Sierra Nevada: A Mountain Journey*. Washington, D.C.: Island Press, 1988.

———. *Stanislaus: The Struggle for a River*. Berkeley: University of California Press, 1981.

———. *The Wild and Scenic Rivers of America*. Washington, D.C.: 1993. Coverage of all rivers designated in the National Wild and Scenic Rivers system.

Palmer, Tim, and William Neill. *Yosemite: The Promise of Wildness*. El Portal: Yosemite Association, 1994. Fine photos by William Neill with Tim Palmer's text about Yosemite National Park.

Restore Hetch Hetchy. *Restore Hetch Hetchy: Feasibility Study*. Sonora, Calif.: Restore Hetch Hetchy, 2005. The case for removing O'Shaughnessy Dam.

Richetts, Taylor H., et al. *Terrestrial Ecoregions of North America*. Washington, D.C.: Island Press, in cooperation with the World Wildlife Fund, 1999. Imperiled species and ecosystems, covered here in chapter 5.

Rose, Gene. *San Joaquin: A River Betrayed*. Fresno: Linrose Publishing Co., 1992. The story of water development.

Runte, Alfred. *Yosemite: The Embattled Wilderness*. Lincoln: University of Nebraska Press, 1990. A history of Yosemite National Park.

Sanborn, Margaret. *Yosemite: Its Discovery, Its Wonders, and Its People*. New York: Random House, 1981.

Schoenherr, Allan A. *A Natural History of California*. Berkeley: University of California Press, 1992. Lightning, sequoias, Clark's nutcrackers, and other natural history.

Sierra Nevada Alliance. "Sierra Foothills of Tulare County Facing 'New Town' Madness." *Sierra News*, June 2006, p. 3. New development proposal, covered here in chapter 5.

———. *Planning for the Future: A Sierra Nevada Land Use Index*. South Lake Tahoe: Sierra Nevada Alliance, 2005. Old-growth remaining (p. 16); local plans inadequate (pp. iv, 24), covered here in chapter 5.

———. *Sierra Climate Change Toolkit*. South Lake Tahoe: Sierra Nevada Alliance, 2005. Global warming and reduction of snowpack (pp. 8–9).

Smith, Genny Schumacher. *Deepest Valley*. Los Altos: William Kaufmann, 1978. Natural history of the eastern Sierra.

Storer, Tracy I., Robert L. Usinger, and David Lukas. *Sierra Nevada Natural History*. Berkeley: University of California Press, 2004.

Strong, Douglas H. *Tahoe: An Environmental History*. Lincoln: University of Nebraska Press, 1984.

Timmer, Kerri L. *Troubled Water of the Sierra*. South Lake Tahoe: Sierra Nevada Alliance, 2003. Water quality and data on U.S. population growth.

van Wagtendonk, Jan. "Fire and Fuel in a Sierra Nevada Ecosystem." http://biology.usgs.gov/s+t/SNT/noframe/ca163.htm (accessed May 31, 2007). Frequency of fires in the Sierra, covered here in chapter 5.

U.S. Geological Survey. "Background, Fire and Fire Surrogate Study, Sequoia National Park Site." www.werc.usgs.gov/fire/seki/ffs/background.htm (accessed May 31, 2007). Catastrophic fires are now worse.

For an extensive list of organizations
involved with the Sierra Nevada,
contact the Sierra Nevada Alliance.

California Wilderness Coalition
1212 Broadway, Suite 1700, Oakland, CA 94612
510 451-1450
www.calwild.org

California Wild Heritage Campaign
916 442-3155
www.californiawild.org

Friends of the River
915 20th St., Sacramento, CA 95814
916 442-3155
www.friendsoftheriver.org

League to Save Lake Tahoe
955 Emerald Bay Road, South Lake Tahoe, CA 96150
530 541-5388
www.keeptahoeblue.org

The Nature Conservancy
201 Mission St., 4th floor, San Francisco, CA 94105
415 777-0487
www.tnccalifornia.org

Planning and Conservation League
1107 9th St., Suite 360, Sacramento, CA 95814
916 444-8726
www.pcl.org

Restore Hetch Hetchy
P.O. Box 3538, Sonora, CA 95370
209 533-4481
www.hetchhetchy.org

Sierra Club, California Chapter (with groups throughout the Sierra)
1414 K St., #500, Sacramento, CA 95814
916 557-1100
www.sierraclubcalifornia.org

Sierra Nevada Alliance
P.O. Box 7989, South Lake Tahoe, CA 96158
530 542-4546
www.sierranevadaalliance.org

South Yuba River Citizens League
216 Main St., Nevada City, CA 95959
530 265-5961
www.yubariver.org

Tuolumne River Trust
Fort Mason Center, Building C, San Francisco, CA 94123
415 292-3531
www.tuolumne.org

Wilderness Society
P. O. Box 29241, San Francisco, CA 94129
415 561-6641
www.wilderness.org

Yosemite Association
P.O. Box 230, El Portal, CA 95318
209 379-2646
www.yosemite.org

RED FIR

Lichen-covered red fir trees excel in upper elevations of
the Sierra's timber zone. This grove borders Long Meadow,
in the San Joaquin basin northeast of Oakhurst.

My wife, Ann Vileisis, participated in this book's creation in every way. She edited several drafts of the manuscript, served as a sounding board for ideas, and enthusiastically joined me on Sierra Nevada trails and rivers, including our four-hundred-mile hike, with all its challenges and rewards. I simply could not do what I do without Ann's love and support.

Steve Medley, director of the Yosemite Association for many years, encouraged me to develop my proposal, and he intended to put his significant talents to work publishing this book as well. After Steve's tragic death in a car accident, the association's publishing committee wisely assigned the production of my book to Malcolm Margolin and his superb publishing company, Heyday Books. Malcolm, editorial director Jeannine Gendar, production editor Diane Lee, and all of the Heyday staff embraced my project and produced *Luminous Mountains* with the skill and experience of a truly professional team. I was especially fortunate to have the master of book design—David Bullen—assigned to my project. Beth Pratt of the Yosemite Association did all that was needed during the critical time of transition.

I appreciate financial support provided to the Yosemite Association and to me from John and Patty Brissenden of Sorensen's Resort in Hope Valley (with assistance of the Sierra Fund), and also from Bert Kerstetter, Becky and Steve Schmitz, and Catherine, Paul, and David Armington. Yvon Chouinard and his company, Patagonia, helped me to buy my new van, which was critical to my travel and work.

Jan van Wagtendonk of the U.S. Geological Survey read the entire manuscript with a critical eye honed by his lifetime as a scientist in the Sierra Nevada. Jerry Meral, formerly of the Planning and Conservation League of California and a lifelong Sierra enthusiast, read each chapter. Joan Clayburgh of the Sierra Nevada Alliance checked my work with her irreplaceable Sierra-wide perspective. Nat Hart and Vicki Graham read my draft copy and commented as only veteran English professors—and great friends—can do. The expert botanical illustrator Linda Ann Vorobik helped me with identification of Sierra wildflowers that appear in my photos.

Janet Cohen harbored our van while Ann and I were on our extended backpacking trip. Bill and Robin Center provided us with a place to camp when we needed it along the American River. John and Patty Brissenden of Sorensen's Resort provided special accommodations to us. Steve Brougher helped us with food delivery on our extended hike, though I am more indebted to this warmhearted friend for his decades of impressive insight, commitment, and activism to keep the Sierra wild.

For a whole lifetime of support on the pathways that count the most, I endlessly appreciate my mother, Jane Palmer May. I also thank her husband, Chuck May, for being the fine man that he is and for his help in large and small ways. It's difficult to imagine a more ardent Yosemite enthusiast than my brother, Jim Palmer, who joined me on a number of Sierra trips through the years.

Journalist Gene Rose was always an inspiration and a friend, and I thank all the other fine reporters and authors who have done outstanding work. A select list appears in my bibliography.

RAINBOW OVER BAILEY RIDGE, WEST OF RANCHERIA CREEK, NORTHERN YOSEMITE
A stormy evening ended with this rainbow as the sun set in the Sierra backcountry.

PAGE NUMBERS WITH ASTERISKS REFER TO PHOTOGRAPHS.

Rivers of America (Harry N. Abrams, 2006), featuring 200 color photos of rivers nationwide, including many in the Sierra Nevada

California Wild (Voyageur, 2004), winner of the 2004 Benjamin Franklin Award for best book on nature and the environment

Lifelines: The Case for River Conservation (Rowman and Littlefield, 2004)

Oregon: Preserving the Spirit and Beauty of Our Land (Voyageur, 2003)

Pacific High: Adventures in the Coast Ranges from Baja to Alaska (Island Press, 2002)

The Heart of America: Our Landscape, Our Future (Island Press, 1999), winner of the 2000 Independent Publisher Book Award for best essay and travel book

America by Rivers (Island Press, 1998)

The Columbia (Mountaineers Books, 1997), winner of the 1998 National Outdoor Book Award

Yosemite: The Promise of Wildness (Yosemite Association, 1994, with William Neill), winner of the 1997 National Park Service Director's Award for best book about a national park.

The Wild and Scenic Rivers of America (Island Press, 1993)

California's Threatened Environment (editor, for the Planning and Conservation League; Island Press, 1992)

The Snake River: Window to the West (Island Press, 1991)

The Sierra Nevada: A Mountain Journey (Island Press, 1988)

Endangered Rivers and the Conservation Movement (University of California Press, 1986)

Youghiogheny: Appalachian River (University of Pittsburgh Press, 1984)

Stanislaus: The Struggle for a River (University of California Press, 1982)

Rivers of Pennsylvania (Pennsylvania State University Press, 1980)

TIM PALMER has written seventeen books about the American landscape, rivers, conservation, and adventure travel. His *California Wild*, a book of text and color photos, won the Benjamin Franklin Award as the best book on nature and the environment in 2004. The National Park Service honored his *Yosemite: The Promise of Wildness* with the Director's Award for the best book about a national park in 1997. Tim edited *California's Threatened Environment*, which was widely used in college classrooms across the state.

About Tim's earlier book *The Sierra Nevada: A Mountain Journey,* the *Washington Post* wrote, "Cool, clean holistic . . . the best single-source record we have of daily Sierra life and the spectrum of regional views on environmental issues. Palmer treks on foot throughout the range, sporting a knowledge of natural history and serving up his own exquisite poetry of light, space and rock. . . . The whole effect is exhilarating."

Recognizing his accumulated contributions in writing and photography, the American Rivers organization gave Tim its first Lifetime Achievement Award in 1988. In 2002 California's Friends of the River recognized him with its highest honor, the Peter Behr Award. *Paddler* magazine named him one of the ten greatest river conservationists of our time, and in 2000 included him as one of the "100 greatest paddlers of the century." In 2005 Tim received the Distinguished Alumni Award from the College of Arts and Architecture at Pennsylvania State University.

Tim has traveled extensively, photographing the Sierra by foot and on skis, from his canoe and whitewater raft. He frequently speaks and gives slide shows at universities, outdoor clubs, workshops, and conferences nationwide. He can be reached at tim@timpalmer.org.

YOSEMITE ASSOCIATION

HEYDAY BOOKS

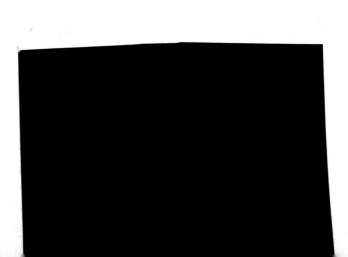